AF439073

PURSUIT

PURSUIT

Bernie Ziegner

PURSUIT
© 2024 By Bernie Ziegner All rights reserved.

No part of this publication may be reproduced, distributed, or transmitted in any form or by any means, including photocopying, recording, or other electronic or mechanical methods, without the prior written permission of the copyright owner and the publisher, except in the case of brief quotations embodied in critical reviews and certain other noncommercial uses permitted by copyright law.

ISBN: 979-8-89021-529-1 Paperback
ISBN: 979-8-89021-530-7 Hardback
ISBN: 979-8-89021-528-4 eBook

Printed in the United States of America.

PURSUIT

A novel by B. Ziegner

Bob Stehling was at loose ends. With his long marriage finished and his career ended by corporate downsizing, he pulled up roots and set out, driving west in his truck camper to visit his cousin in Montana, and with no plans beyond that. Violence, romance and mob interests merge on the Midwest highways when Bob's life was suddenly and irrevocably changed. Violence and danger find Bob at Timberline Ranch, where a new purpose and value for life gives Bob the strength to fight for those he came to care for.

CONTENTS

CHAPTER 1 MOVING ON

Bob took the Dunkin' Donuts cup out of the holder and shook it. Empty. He put it back and then glanced at the fuel gauge. A hair over half full.

The sign came up quickly: *Rest Stop, Full Service, 2 miles.*

"Perfect," he mumbled, but wondered what kind of coffee he'd have to put up with, not likely Dunkin' Donuts.

It was late morning as Bob Stehling approached Albany and parked at the rest stop. The large cup of coffee had lasted him from Lowell, Massachusetts. A half hour without coffee was about his limit; so that would have to be first, then the fuel tank.

He closed the door, ran his hand over the warm hood and smiled to himself, pleased with the new 2005 Dodge pickup truck. It handled well, he thought, even with the heavy camper he had installed the previous week. The wind resistance of the cab-over camper would keep his gas mileage down; but he was determined to live with it.

Bob went into the service building, stopped at the men's room, and then walked into the food court. The Burger King was at the far end. He shook his head as he looked at the menu board above the counter. *Oh, what the hell. Cholesterol be damned,* he thought, *I'm hungry.*

Two men in front of him playfully jostled each other as they waited their turn. Both had *DiLorean Moving* stenciled on the back of their green coveralls. One glanced back, saw Bob, but continued to talk to his partner. Bob could hear both well.

"Gonna drop some of our load in Gary," said the older man, standing to Bob's left. "Shouldn't take more than an hour."

"Gary?" His friend sounded incredulous. "Who the hell moves to Gary?"

The older man chuckled. "What the hell, it'll give us room to pick up something in Rockford."

"We gotta haul this load clear to Boise. What're we gonna do with anything extra?"

"Not to worry. We'll do a 'rest stop' in Salt Lake, lose it there." The man emphasized the *rest stop* with his fingers.

"This whole thing makes me nervous," said the younger man, lowering his voice. "We get seen by the wrong person and we're screwed."

"Quit worrying."

The line moved up and the men placed their order. Then it was Bob's turn.

Bob walked back to the truck, puzzling over the overheard conversation. *Didn't sound legal to me…whatever it was,* he mused. *Maybe moving some hot merchandise?* Back in the truck, he relaxed and enjoyed his lunch, surprised and pleased the coffee was better than expected.

His initial nervousness and uncertainty about pulling up roots in his fifties and leaving home had abated considerably since early morning. He looked forward to the trip, anxious to see things he had only heard of or visited vicariously through the TV. His whole life had been lived in or near the city of Lowell, and he had only dreams of distant places. The phone call from his cousin in Montana convinced him that he would be welcome at the guest ranch his cousin called home. He'd stop there first, he decided.

There was mostly mundane chatter by truck drivers on the CB radio as he went across Massachusetts. Bob kept the radio on channel 19, hoping to get an early warning from truckers about the presence of police cruisers, detours, and road hazards. Comfortably sipping his coffee, he became aware of a loud nearby signal screaming over the chatter.

"Fred, got your ears on? Leo here. Come back."

"Hey Leo, loud an clear. Must be close."

"Comin' up on your six. Gotcha in sight. Got company?"

"Nah, all alone," Fred responded. "What's up with you? Can you move up 4 and set it on low-power? Lots of interference on this channel."

"Roger. Movin' up now."

Suddenly there was only the cacophony of background signals. Fred and Leo were gone. *Huh? Movin' up? What did that mean?* Then he thought of something he had heard earlier and, on a hunch, reached for the channel selector. He turned it from 19 to 23, and resumed listening.

"…heading for Rockford, then points west," said Leo.

"Fred, you still on track for ah…Lawndale?"

"Roger that. Talked to the man earlier on the landline. It's all set."

"Great. I'll be comin' in behind you. The man doesn't want stuff lying around…got to move it."

"Understood," said Fred. "Hey, you runnin' empty?"

"Picked up half a load this morning, but plenty of room for, ah, anything else."

"We'll get together for a cold one on my way back, Leo."

"10-4. See you then."

The radio went silent. Bob set the channel selector back to 19, but there was just the usual humdrum chatter. *What the hell was that all about? Second time I heard about Rockford in the last half hour.* He checked channel 23 again, nothing, and turned it back to 19. Bob kept playing the conversation over and over in his head.

—

Fred Bucari had waited until the swing-shift left at midnight, leaving him and Al Salerno, the shift boss, alone to load the extra pallets of automotive components into the available trailer space. There was usually a mystery load going somewhere, Fred mused; items Al had secreted in the warehouse from skimming certain high value shipments. He didn't know how Al accounted for the losses and he just as soon not be told. *The less I know the better,* he thought.

"There'll be a few bucks waiting for ya when this load gets to Rockford," said Al, grinning.

"Well, today I've got the space; might as well use it, huh?"

"Your manifest usually calls for a full load, and I gotta *jam* my stuff in there," said Al. "Today is easy."

"Dispatch wanted me to get this stuff on the road. They knew it wasn't quite full."

"Lucky break. I can put *all* my stuff for Rockford in there," said Al.

"I think they have a cranky customer in Milwaukee that wanted his shipment in a hurry and was willing to pay."

"Did you do a good sweep for bugs in the trailer?" asked Al raising an eyebrow. "You're on their shit list, you know."

Fred nodded. "There's nothing inside it. I'm sure of that. And, I just inspected every inch of the outside."

Al pointed to the tractor cab. "You got that damn data radio up there. You be careful when you talk on the CB 'case they got you wired for sound."

"Hadn't thought of that." Fred shook his head. "Shit."

"Just be careful." Al handed the two manifests to Fred. "Paper work is in order. Keep the phony copy visible. Hide the real one until you leave Rockford."

Fred looked at the paperwork and nodded. "Okay."

Al worked the forklift himself and put the extra pallets in the trailer. Opaque plastic wrap secured the shipments.

Fred had inspected the trailer earlier for security sensors, cameras or recording devices. The unit seemed clean, nothing suspicious. He knew that Al had rendered the cameras on the loading dock inoperable. Fred grinned. *Seems like there is always something going wrong with them.*

He had to be careful, now more than ever, Fred thought. He had 'lost' partial loads of high-end goods in the past. He wasn't fooling anybody. He'd just been lucky and not been caught. The R&R Freight company inspectors had spot-checked the seals on the trailer doors on more than one occasion. Unable to explain the losses, he had been suspended pending an investigation. The company detectives were unable to solve the losses, and the union helped him get reinstated. But now there was a data radio and GPS unit on top of the cab to keep an accurate tally of his time and mileage, and let the home office computer know his whereabouts. *But still*, he thought, *where there's a will, there's a way.* The freight loss was now occurring at the warehouses, and Fred merely delivered it along his route.

Fred walked around the rig and checked the tires and air hoses. Anxious to get rolling, he looked at his watch and then checked the seals on the trailer doors. He was up on the dock and into the office just as Al hung up the phone "You're all set, Fred. I just told Tim what you're bringing him. Shouldn't be any problem with the paperwork."

"Thanks. I better get goin'."

Al nodded. "Have a good trip."

Fred jumped off the loading dock and climbed into the cab. He looked again at the two manifests. It seemed like a clean and simple operation. When he had talked with Tim O'Brien earlier, Tim had mentioned that he was anxious to get the pallets of replacement parts for Audi, Mercedes and Volvo cars, because he had customers waiting.

Fred put the truck in gear and started for the gate. He should be in Rockford in a day and a half and the two-grand payoff he was promised would sure come in handy. In the meantime, he had to get out of Hartford and make his way up to Kingston on the NY Thruway. He had a small load to deliver at a plastics company before heading up to Albany. Then it was hammer down on I-90, stop in Rockford, and continue to his main drop.

At the fuel islands, Bob tossed the bag of lunch trash into a garbage bin then selected the fuel pump. The ever increasing cost of gasoline was unsettling. He felt sure the price would go even higher. He seethed at the thought.

It's not like the country didn't have a warning. Shit, 1973 should have been a wake-up call, Bob thought as he filled the tank. He felt himself getting agitated, as was usual when he pondered the state of affairs in the country.

"Nope, the opportunity was wasted. ... Bastards," he said to no one in particular.

He finished fueling, grabbed his receipt, and went to clean the windshield. He grumbled about the oil and automobile companies. Then he turned his attention to the administration and politicians in general.

"NAFTA, CAFTA, crapta! More jobs lost in the U.S.A and more exploited workers in Mexico and Central America."

He shook his head and tossed the window squeegee into the receptacle and got back into his truck. He turned on the radio and found a station with 'The Music of Your Life,' a syndicated program in a world he understood and was comfortable in. He accelerated onto the highway and turned up the volume as Andy Williams began his rendition of *Moon River.*

Bob would miss his friends. He thought back at his parting that morning.

"You shoulda had a garage sale," Roy said, laughing. "Look at all this crap."

His wife poked her elbow into his ribs.

He saw her scowl. "What?"

"It's all he's got left." Amy said in a voice too low for Bob to hear.

Bob lay a stack of 33-rpm vinyl records on top of a bookcase. Then one last look at his belongings and lowered the overhead door of the U-Store unit. Roy and his wife watched him put the padlock through the door clasp.

Bob grinned. "Everything is boxed up. The shipper can just pick up this crap when I'm ready for it." He tossed Roy the key to the storage unit.

"Stuff'll be here when you get back," said Amy.

Roy looked at the key in his palm for a moment. "Let us know how you're doing, okay?" He shook his head. "Damn, I still can't believe you're leaving."

"I'll send an e-mail when I can. Don't worry about the stuff in the locker. I'll let you know if I need it, then I'll hire some outfit to ship it."

Bob shook hands with Roy, then turned and hugged Amy. "Thanks for everything."

"You take care of yourself." She wiped her cheek with the back of her hand. "Call us if you get in trouble."

Bob nodded and climbed into the cab. The three of them had lived in Lowell all their lives and attended the same schools. Roy had gone on to college and now owned an insurance agency.

Like his father, Bob had become a machinist and spent most of his career at the B&M maintenance depot. But now at only 53, he had retired, albeit with some help from corporate downsizing. No one wanted to hire a man his age in this new economy.

"Bye, guys," he called out as he started moving out of the storage lot.

One last wave and he turned toward the southbound entrance ramp for US-3.

Roy returned the wave. "I still can't believe it. It just ain't him."

Amy nodded a few times. "He's got to get it out of his system. He'll be back."

Bob felt odd and a bit sad leaving the place where he had lived all his life. He wondered if he would come to regret it. For sure, he would miss Roy and Amy, lifelong friends. But, now well into his fifties, Bob's roots no longer held tightly to the town and his old life. His mid-40s lady friend of the last several months had succumbed to the lure of a man half her age, his ex-wife had moved to Ft. Lauderdale with a real-estate developer a year ago, and his son was working in a big law firm in Atlanta. Sure, he received a telephone call from him on the holidays and e-mail now and then, but otherwise he hadn't seen him or the grandkids in over two years.

—

Bob hadn't heard from his cousin Ralph Stehling in Montana for almost a year. Recently, however, Bob had written him for his birthday and asked about visiting on his way west. Ralph, 55-years old, lived with his wife and daughter at the Timberline Ranch in Elk Creek, and telephoned when he received Bob's card.

"Bob! How the heck are you? It's been a while."

"Sure has. Haven't seen you since Las Vegas. What was that, ten years ago?" asked Bob.

"Damn, you're right. Ten years."

"I'm heading out your way; wondered if I could drop in and visit?"

"Damn straight, you *better* stop here. What are you up to these days?" asked Ralph.

"I want to get out of New England."

"You lived there all your life. You're gonna just up and leave?"

"There isn't anything holding me here any longer. Not a damn thing."

"So where you going on this trip of yours?" asked Ralph.

"I haven't really made any plans. I'll stop and see you and then go visit the National Parks in the Northwest. I have a few friends in Oregon."

"I can't believe that you gave up your apartment and put all your stuff in storage. And you're going to ride around and do what...write stories?" Ralph sounded incredulous.

"Yeah, I have to do this...change direction...now or never," Bob responded. They had talked for nearly an hour and Ralph extended a warm welcome to his cousin.

Bob hadn't been able to find Elk Creek on the Rand-McNally road atlas, but did see that Camden, the county seat Ralph had mentioned, was located up against the Bitterroot Mountains along the Idaho – Montana border. He would head there first, and from there he would probably visit the National Parks as he drifted toward the West Coast. It was a long way, he thought; the better part of a week. But, he was in no hurry.

CHAPTER 2 DINNER CHATTER

Bob kept it at the speed limit along the I-90 New York Thruway. The signs indicated 275 miles between Albany and Buffalo. He found it an easy road to travel, passing through pleasant rolling country of small towns and farms, and along the Erie Canal and Mohawk River. He tried to recall his history lessons of the colonial times and the stories of the Erie Canal. Well before reaching Lake Erie, the country changed from rolling hills and farms to flat terrain with grape orchards. Bob hadn't realized that the land bordering the Great Lakes was grape and wine country. *Learn something new every day,* he mused.

It was late afternoon when Bob decided to stop for supper. The homeward rush of I-90 traffic around Buffalo was heavy, and he looked forward to a break. Spotting a billboard for *Jerry's Diner, Truck Parking*, he drove onto the off-ramp and paid his toll.

"Gotta pay another damn toll. But hell, I'm tired and hungry."

Many trucks were parked behind the diner, and cars filled the side parking lot. He hoped to be able to find a seat. Luckily there was an empty stool at the counter, and he squeezed in between two burly men.

The dinner specials were posted on a small blackboard above the counter, and while he stared at it, a waitress came by.

"Start with coffee, hon?"

"Sure." He looked back at the menu board.

The waitress brought a heavy mug with steaming coffee and several prepackaged creamers. "Need a few minutes?"

"All set."

She pulled an order pad out of her uniform pocket.

"I'd like the chicken-fried steak special."

"Comes with mashed and string beans."

He nodded. "Sounds fine."

She smiled and took the order slip to the pass-through window. He looked at her; a middle-aged woman who had not had an easy life, he decided. Crow's feet bordered her eyes and her mouth. Her hands were wrinkled, fingers thin. A simple wedding band was on her finger. Her shoulders were slightly stooped. He liked her face. Her soft eyes spoke of kindness.

When the big man to his right got up to leave, Bob looked around casually. The place was filled with truck drivers, a few older couples, maybe retired, and a young couple in animated conversation. The older people were dressed nicely, maybe a bit too much for this place, he thought. They didn't talk much, just an occasional comment to each other. The truck drivers to his left seemed intent on their meals. There was occasional conversation, which touched mostly on their route and schedule. Bob listened to their chatter, curious as to what their lives were like. Then his ears perked up.

"I gotta stop in Rockford tomorrow," said the driver next to him.

Bob could barely hear the other driver respond. "Shit, you still doing that? Not me, man."

"Yeah, easy money."

"Can't spend it in Joliet."

"A couple more times and I'll have my rig paid for."

Bob heard the other driver mumble, "Get out of it while you still can."

"Yeah, I hear ya."

The waitress brought Bob a small fresh salad and he ate it with gusto, pleased it wasn't the wilted lettuce he often experienced in diners. He hadn't had chicken fried steak in several years, and he enjoyed this platter even though it was smothered in gravy he mostly swept aside.

The two drivers got up from the counter and walked to the cashier. *Rockford. What the hell's in Rockford?* Bob tried to recall the earlier conversations. *Some nefarious activity,* he wondered?

A slice of cherry pie was not a disappointment and he asked for more coffee. The waitress dropped his check on the counter and thanked him with a smile. Bob left a good tip.

He slid into the truck seat and closed the door, glad he hadn't settled for a quick burger at a fast food place. Bob merged into the swollen evening traffic heading south from Buffalo along Lake Erie on westbound I-90. U-Haul trucks, sometimes with a car in tow, passed him occasionally. This time he saw a middle aged couple, unsmiling, and he wondered if they had recently lost their jobs or maybe even their home. He shook his head in sympathy.

The sun had dropped below the treetops as Bob entered Pennsylvania. He hadn't seen a truck stop for an hour and he was tired. His lower back had started to pain him. When he saw a sign pointing to camping facilities, he turned off the expressway, paid the toll, and followed the signs to the campground at the edge of Lake Erie where the expanse of water swept out to the horizon. *An inland ocean*, he thought. He realized that he had never seen Lake Erie, although decades ago he had been to Niagara Falls.

He pulled into Peterson's Lakeside Campground and registered. The campground held a preponderance of large RV units with older couples sitting in lawn chairs or at wooden picnic tables. These folks had done well and made a comfortable livelihood, he thought, before the age of selfishness, and avarice descended on the country. A few tent campers, with hardy looking young couples were setting up for their evening meal at the fire grills. Bob made the electrical connection to the camper. Inside he prepared his four-cup coffee maker and sat down at the table with his laptop computer. He thought about his e-mail, but decided that he would look at it at some other time, maybe at the end of the week. While sipping his coffee, he entered his thoughts for the day into his travel log, ideas for his novel. *What was all that stuff on the CB? What the hell is in Rockford?*

CHAPTER 3 LAWNDALE DINER

Bob broke camp at 8 a.m and stopped for fuel and a breakfast snack at a general store a mile back toward the highway. Locals, all greeting the cashier by name, came in to buy a newspaper and pick up food items. Bob paid for the fuel, bought pastry and a large coffee to go.

He was on I-90 by 8:30 headed for Cleveland, hoping to get past Chicago by evening. A long *day*, he thought, *lots of traffic*. Bob smiled, the weather was sunny, just some high wispy clouds. The traffic on the Interstate was heavy with nearly as many trucks as cars. Bob found himself in a nervous state of alert with the constant flow of trucks, the road repair activity, and with cars that were being driven well past the speed limit and weaving between the trucks - the morning rush.

He listened to local programs on the radio, the hourly newscasts, and occasionally an oldies station. Otherwise, Bob kept the radio off and the CB on Channel 19 with the volume low. He thought about his hopes for the future, wanting to see the country, and maybe staying in some places for an extended time to get a better feel of the land and its people, and to be able to write about them.

Bob looked forward to seeing his cousin again. He remembered Ralph's wife, Susan, but had only a faint recollection of their daughter, Liz. She was twenty years old now and going to college. He doubted that he would recognize her. Of course, he had aged, too, he thought. He hoped that visiting Ralph would turn out okay, and that he wouldn't be a burden. *I'll play it by ear*, he thought. He felt some hesitancy in staying with his cousin at the ranch; after all, it was a guest ranch and not exactly a place where one just dropped in. He didn't want his presence to become a problem with the owner. The idea of staying there appealed to him though, and he thought about it often. It would be very different from anything that he had ever done; maybe something he could write about.

Bob arrived in Toledo before noon and stopped for fuel. He filled up his coffee mug and returned to the truck with and a chicken sandwich. Relaxing in the sun-warmed cab felt good. He watched the flow of people come and go from the rest stop and wondered what their lives were about. Sometimes it was easy; a girl in a small car loaded with clothes and a college decal in the back window. Other times he wasn't so sure; an old station wagon loaded to the windows with possessions, clothes and toys. Kids in the back. A harried looking middle aged couple in the front. Bob hesitated to draw any conclusions, but feared these were displaced people, people that had lost their livelihood, nomads.

—

The breakfast crowd had left, and Lillian sat down for toast and coffee. Vinny was on a rampage again. *What an asshole*, she thought. She regretted having come here to work. Her ex-husband, Joey, Vinny's cousin, had insisted; his paranoia evident in wanting to keep an eye on her. The divorce had been difficult and she marveled that she hadn't been killed. She had agreed to live at the Lawndale Diner and open in the morning as part of getting Joey's agreement to a divorce settlement; without agreeing to the diner there wouldn't have been a settlement. With half of the proceeds from the sale of the house and the $100K one-time, she would be able to start again – but it would have to be well away from here, she knew. The lawyer she had hired was expensive, but worth every dollar.

Lillian knew that Vinny would be more of a watchman for Joey than an employer; but for a little while, she would have to bear it. She would make plans – plans to be rid of them all. She had lived in fear of Joey and his mob crew for years, but that would end. It would take some time - if only she could keep Vinny at bay.

She hadn't known Vinny that well because Joey had kept his crew away from the house. But now, she realized how vile and dangerous Vinny really was. He had no respect for her, probably reflecting Joey's attitude. Vinny often groped her in passing, accompanied by lewd humor. He pressured her to work in his strip club, getting angry when she always declined. If she talked back to him during his sudden and often violent rages, he would swing at her with a painful bruising slap. He reveled in humiliating her in front of Jimmy, the teenage dish washer. She loathed Vinny but resisted the urge to drive a knife into his gut. Her turn would come.

This is not going to be a good day, she thought. He was yelling about something. She got up from the booth and took her plates to the dish cart.

She heard Vinny roar from the kitchen. "Lillian!"

Her hair bristled on the back of her neck.

—

The R&R truck left I-90 at the Rockford, IL toll booth. Fred Bucari drove toward town and turned into the Lawndale Truck Wash and Warehouse located a few hundred feet behind the diner. He was expected to make his first delivery in Milwaukee that night and then go on to Minneapolis in the morning. He pulled into the truck wash entrance and stopped. He'd let the crew take it through while he ate supper. He jotted down the time and miles on his log, knowing that the data radio on the roof already gave his position and time to the Newark office. *Hell, I'm stopping at a diner aren't I? Gotta eat.*

He got out of the truck, stretched, and then went to the service window. He handed a credit card to the attendant for the washing charges, and signed the receipt. When he knocked on the door marked 'OFFICE', a burly man opened it, blocked the doorway, and just stared at him. The man behind him at the desk looked up and smiled. The plaque on the desk read *Terry O'Brian.*

"Good to see ya, Fred. Come on in. No trouble, I guess?"

"Nah, easy ride."

The big guy at the doorway stepped aside. Tim tossed an envelope to Fred, who caught it easily, looked inside, and then stuffed it into his vest pocket.

"Get yourself some dinner. We'll have your rig bright and shiny when you come back."

Fred smiled, patted the envelope in his vest pocket, and said "Thanks, Tim. I *am* hungry."

Fred walked across the parking lot to the diner. *The extra $2000 will sure come in handy,* he told himself. *Half-hour should be long enough for them to remove the extra pallets and mold new seals. Yeah, these guys are experts.* The interior of the truck wash was not visible from outside when the doors were closed. Few knew that the interior walls on the warehouse side of the building rolled open, and a hydraulically operated platform could be moved to the trailer doors, and the extra loads removed in only a few minutes. The false manifest would be destroyed, new seals would be counterfeited and attached, and the truck would reappear from the exit door dripping water, sparkling clean, and just slightly lighter. Fred had been shown the small operation in the back of the building where a retired machinist made quick tooling for each new seal using a sacrificial casting method. [Can you explain what that is for us dumb readers?] The original seal would be enclosed in a moldable ceramic to copy the physical features. The ceramic would be dried, separated into halves, and the original seal removed. The ceramic halves would be heated to improve strength before being joined and liquid metal poured into the mold. *Damn slick operation*, he thought.

Fred had transported hot loads before and no one had challenged him. He knew other guys brought stuff into this warehouse. Once in a while he heard that a driver got busted by an insurance spot check, but he'd been careful and kept a tight lip on his own activity. There was always a finite risk, however, and he feared he would get tripped up on some unforeseen event. It was getting riskier all the time. The shippers and insurance companies were getting smarter, but he'd kept up with them, so far. On the Internet he had found all the information he needed about the security methods that were being implemented by trucking companies. Just a couple more years, he thought, and then he could ditch the whole thing and retire. He had pulled it off before, a few months ago with a cargo of high-end bathroom sinks and fixtures. It had netted him an easy $1500. *Bathroom fixtures - who would have thought?* He grinned to himself as he entered the diner. He *was* hungry.

The sun was well into the western sky as Bob approached Chicago. He checked his map to make sure that he took the route well to the west of the city, away from the crippling evening traffic on the Ryan Expressway, a situation friends had cautioned him about. An hour later he was on I-39 northbound toward Rockford where he intended to pick up I-90 again.

He listened to the CB and paid attention to the chatter of the truck drivers, listening for any road or traffic hazards ahead. Several times he heard mention of the Lawndale Diner. He recalled the conversation he had overheard the day before, and the mention of Rockford and Lawndale. The drivers on the CB said the food was just fair, but they had really good-sized portions and one wouldn't go hungry. One driver said the waitress was a real looker. That brought several acknowledgments.

Bob understood from the radio chatter that many truckers parked their rigs overnight in the big parking lot between the diner and truck wash. Several drivers had gotten into a heated discussion questioning the safety of using the truck wash service. Two drivers mentioned having been approached in the diner about participating in a "profitable" cargo arrangement. The drivers had not gone back there again. Other drivers claimed no such problem. Bob, intrigued, decided to stop at the Lawndale Diner for supper. After all, he had to eat somewhere. Maybe there was something there he could use in a novel.

When the sign for Rockford, Illinois, appeared, Bob exited and turned toward the town, pulling into the parking lot of the Lawndale Diner at 4 p.m. He angled into a parking spot alongside the classic 1950s metal building that offered an easy way to get back to the street. Toward the rear of the diner, he could see the back of the Lawndale Truck Wash and Warehouse, about 200 feet away. Several trailer trucks were parked in the large asphalt area and two trucks waited at the truck wash entrance. Steam and spray emanated from the entrance. There was a truck backed to the loading dock at the warehouse. *Looks rather tame. I'll go in and get a meal, good a place as any. Don't look very busy, but then it isn't really dinner hour yet.*

As Bob entered, an older couple left. They thanked him, for holding the door. The grating sound of the loud jukebox invaded his senses. A man wearing coveralls walked past him toward the doorway, an R&R Trucking emblem on his baseball hat, the name Fred stitched over his chest. *Maybe the same Fred I heard on the radio?* Bob saw a raucous group of youngsters taking up two corner booths at the far end, with older couples in two other booths closer to the door. A middle-aged waitress ambled toward the youngsters. *Probably kids who come in after school every day*, he thought.

The counter was empty and Bob took a seat facing the pass-through window. An attractive waitress came around the corner from the kitchen, at the far end of the counter. *Wow, the drivers hadn't been kidding.* She smiled at Bob, pulled a menu from a pocket at the end of the counter and handed it to him. He glanced at her name tag, Lillian. He met her glance and smiled. She returned the smile but seemed nervous and glanced towards the pass-through window from where a low mumbling voice was coming. The *thump-thump-thump* of the jukebox music was irritating. Annoyed, Bob glanced at the crowd in the corner booths.

"Oh, they're in here after school nearly every day. Maria might get three bucks tip if she's lucky."

He turned back to look at Lillian.

"The supper specials are listed inside the menu. Coffee?" she asked.

"Sure. Thanks." *What a nice throaty sound.* He was reminded of Julie London and her torch songs of the 60s and 70s. *Even looks a little like her.*

He looked at the supper specials and then glanced up while she pulled her order pad and a pen from the pocket of the pink uniform. The uniform did nothing to hide her attractive figure. *Maybe forty,* he thought, *damn pretty, though. No rings.* Her brown hair was up in a net, but he envisioned it falling to her shoulder. *A real looker, indeed.* When he raised his eyes to her, she met his gaze, smiling; but then a loud clamor came from the kitchen. She jumped and the smile disappeared.

"Could I have the Salisbury Steak? Mashed and carrots would be great," he volunteered.

"It comes with a small salad." She met his gaze again with a hint of a smile.

He wrinkled his face.

"It's fresh. Really. I cut up the lettuce about a half hour ago."

"Okay."

"Dressing?"

"Just some vinegar and oil."

As she turned, he glanced at her as she poured a mug of coffee, and then set it in front of him. When she leaned over to place the order slip in the pass-through window, he stole another look at her. She straightened some glassware on the shelf, and then went around the corner at the end of the counter into the kitchen.

Bob looked around. The booths and counter were spotless and the area behind the counter was orderly. *She keeps a clean place,* he thought. The afternoon sun lit the interior of the diner, reflecting off the shiny metal surfaces and a tray of fluted water tumblers. Interesting, he thought, that they would still be using the heavy glass tumblers and not some cheap plastic ones. He sipped his coffee. *Goddamn thumpy-ass music.*

Voices from the kitchen could be easily heard through the pass-through window. Someone was yelling, swearing, and pounding a fist on something. Bob put down his coffee mug. The hair on the back of his neck stood up. He listened.

"Joey said you're a stupid woman, and I believe him! You're hardly earning your keep around here. The deal I'm offering you will give you some real dough - you'll be rolling in it. Get smart you prissy little bitch. Use what you got!"

"In your dreams, Vinny. You're disgusting. You put your hands on me again and I'll call the cops." She spoke evenly and clearly.

That is *Lillian*, he thought.

"You'll what?" The voice was loud, an edge of rage in it.

Bob heard what sounded like a hard slap and then a cry. The music didn't mask the sound. He tried to look into the pass-through window but couldn't see anybody.

"Leave her alone, Vinny." That was a different voice, *a boy's voice*, thought Bob.

"You shut up and mind your own business." The words, spat, sounded like a real threat.

Again Bob heard a slap and another cry. There followed a loud crash and the sound of dishes breaking. Bob got up from his seat.

"You clumsy bitch!"

Bob glanced toward the people in the booths. No one seemed to be paying attention. The music was loud. He heard another slap, followed by a scream. Visions of his mother being brutalized came back to Bob. The visions reminded him of his helplessness as a child.

Louise came around the counter to the pass-through window and left an order with a swat at the bell. She turned toward Bob.

"They're always into it." She shook her head and went out toward her booths.

A muffled yell overpowered the noise of a new tune on the jukebox. Alarmed for Lillian, Bob got off his stool and moved toward the end of the counter, looking for some sort of weapon. He picked up a heavy glass bottle filled with what looked like salad oil. He grabbed it by the long neck and held it like a club at his side, turned the corner and stepped into the kitchen entryway.

Broken dishes and food were strewn across the floor near the pass-through and Bob thought he recognized his Salisbury steak supper. The aluminum tray had come to rest by the butcher's block. He looked at a hulk of a man standing with his back to him, his waist wrapped in an apron, a tee shirt covering a barrel chest.

A boy stood with his back against the dishwasher, about as far as he could get from the threatening hulk with a mallet in his upraised fist. As Bob took another step forward, he saw Lillian to his left, her hand raised in front of her face but offering scant protection. Her eyes were fixed on the mallet in the big man's hand. Suddenly the man made a move around the butcher's block toward Lillian. She cried out, moving to keep away from the mallet.

"Vinny! Get away from me!"

Bob quickly stepped up behind him.

"Bitch… What the hell?" He started to turn, as if he sensed someone behind him.

Bob landed the heavy bottle against the back of Vinny's head. The big man dropped to his knees. The mallet skittered across the floor. He then yelled in rage and reached for a knife sitting on the edge of the butcher's block. Without hesitating, Vinny roared incoherently and lunged toward Bob with the knife in the air. Bob sidestepped at the last moment and swung the heavy bottle again, this time smacking it onto the side of his head. The knife clattered to the floor. Time stood still. All was quiet. Then his eyes rolled upward, and his knees buckled. Vinny fell face forward onto the floor with a thud.

The boy stared at Bob, mouth agape. Lillian sobbed, covering her mouth with her hands. Bob looked at Lillian. "Get out! Get out of here now."

She stood frozen.

"Get out! Go!"

With a small cry, she ran to the back of the kitchen and disappeared. Bob could hear her running up the stairs. *Why the hell is she going upstairs? She should get out of here.* His heart was pounding.

"What's your name kid?" Bob looked over at the boy.

"Jimmy. It's Jimmy," he said hesitantly.

"Jimmy, when this guy wakes up, maybe you'd better be somewhere else, like maybe looking for a new job."

"Maybe he's dead." The boy stared at the big man on the floor.

"No. I can see him breathing. He'll have a headache though."

"He didn't have any right to do that, to hurt her. She's a nice person." Jimmy looked like he was going to cry.

"Jimmy, you got someplace to go? Ain't gonna be healthy for you around here no more."

"Yeah, I live with my mom and dad across town. The bastard always had his hands on her. She's a really good person. Been here eight months. Works really hard. Asshole doesn't care, wants her in his strip club."

Bob could see Jimmy's eyes glistening. "Okay, Jimmy. He's out for a while. Why don't you hightail it outa here before dipshit here wakes up."

Jimmy nodded, looking at the prone figure. "He had no right…"

"He's been beating her?" asked Bob.

"Yeah, whenever he gets mad about something. He talks to her like she's trash. She's not."

Just then they heard footsteps rushing down the stairs and Bob caught a glimpse of Lillian as she rushed out of the back door carrying a large shoulder bag and a smaller duffel. The door closed behind her.

Bob checked the big man's breathing and pulse.

"Is he alive?" asked Jimmy hesitantly.

"Sure. Listen kid, you better haul-ass outa here."

"Yeah, I'm going down the street and call my mom from the drugstore." Jimmy bolted past him and out the back door.

Just then Louise appeared. "Holy shit! What happened? Where's Lillian?" She looked down at Vinny. "What'd you do to him?"

"He'll live. Lillian left. The kid too."

"What the hell…I got customers out there!" Louise looked at him with some trepidation.

"He'll come around soon, won't be happy though. I guess you're on your own."

"Shit! I don't need this!" She threw her hands in the air and left the kitchen.

Bob saw the heavy bottle that he had used for a club laying intact on the floor. He picked it up and wiped it down with a wet towel that was on the butcher's block. *No point in leaving my autograph behind.* He set the bottle on a shelf next to a can of corn oil, wiped his hands on the wet towel and tossed it across the room. His heart was racing. He took some deep breaths. *I better get the hell out of here.* He turned to leave the kitchen.

—

Lillian stood trembling at the top of the stairs, trying not to sob. Vinny would kill her, she just knew he would. But a deep anger boiled inside her, an anger that pushed aside her fear, an anger that had festered for months from the hurt and humiliation. She recalled the groping; the foul names he used on her, the degrading comments in front of customers, and she blinked back tears. She turned suddenly and went into his office, rage replaced her good sense. She looked at his desk, rifled through the haphazard array of things next to his computer. She wanted to hurt him, wanted revenge, and then she spotted the safe piled high with papers and junk. The door was slightly ajar.

"You lazy bastard," she mumbled. Vinny rarely kept his safe locked and besides, the lock code was jotted on a Post-it note on the side of the computer. She flung open the safe door and opened several small cloth bags until she found one with bundles of cash. She grabbed the bag, closed the door to the safe and rushed out of the office.

Fear moved in to replace rage. Thinking that Vinny would wake up and trap her, she picked up her bags and hurried down the stairs and out the back door without glancing into the kitchen. She threw her bags into the back seat of her car and then went quickly to start the engine. A loud clicking came from under the hood every time she turned the key. "Oh shit!" she cried. The battery had been giving her trouble for several days, but she had wanted to wait until payday to go to the garage. "No, No," she gasped.

She got out of the car, pulled her bags from the back seat and stood there looking around in panic. She started toward the street and passed the back of the truck camper. Suddenly she realized that the camper belonged to the stranger who had come to her rescue. It had a Massachusetts license plate. She tried to open the door to the camper and to her amazement, the handle turned. The door opened easily. Without thinking, she tossed her bags inside and climbed in. She closed the door and pushed the lock button. Her heart raced, but she hoped the driver would return soon and drive off . . . without looking around. She fervently hoped he would drive her away from here.

—

Fred was pleased with his clean and spray-waxed truck. He climbed into the cab and started the engine. His eyes scanned the gauges then picked up his logbook and entered the time. He needed the entry to be accurate because he knew that the data radio had already broadcast his location to the R&R Trucking office in Newark. Another big trailer was being backed up to the loading dock. Leo was undoubtedly prepared to whisk away the pallets of black market auto goods.

He eased the truck onto the street. *Another hour and a half to Milwaukee,* he thought. *Minneapolis in the morning. Then head to Seattle.* He thought about the great deal of extra money he had made over the last few years, recalling a driver who had approached him while they sat in the diner one night. The guy had made it sound so easy. Indeed it had been, so far. But how long would his luck last? First there had been his daughter's orthodontics, then his wife's knee surgery, and now his daughter was ready to go to college. The extra income had been a godsend, but if he ever got caught, it would destroy his family. He wasn't the only one doing this; the truck wash had been in business for several years. But, what would the reaction be when he decided to quit? He scratched his chin. *Does anyone ever really quit?*

———

Bob heard Vinny moan although the man was not moving. Bob hurried out of the kitchen and almost collided with Louise.

"What should I do?" she gasped. "I've got customers."

"He'll come around soon. Please let me have a coffee - better make it to go, just milk in it."

Louise stared at him and then nodded and went to the coffee urns. She was back quickly and handed him the cup.

"Look, I'm sorry. I just couldn't let that brute lay into her. I hope it doesn't create problems for you."

She looked at him, and then shook her head, resignedly. "I can handle him. He's just a low-life asshole. I'll go in back. I do most of the cooking anyway. He's not here half the time."

A loud roar of laughter came from the corner booths gauge a new jarring tune vibrated the floor. Louise nodded toward them.

"I can fling a few hamburgers together for them. No biggy." She paused, moving her hands nervously. "What…what do I say to Vinny?"

"Nothing, but he'll be rippin' when he wakes up…be careful."

Bob pulled out a fold of bills from his shirt pocket and peeled off a ten.

"Here, I'm taking a Danish with me." He grabbed the pastry from under the transparent cover.

Louise looked at the ten in her hand and glance up at him.

"Keep it. I'm gone, headed to Montana."

CHAPTER 4 ESCAPE

Bob moved through the diner, pushed open the door, and breathed deep of the cool air. He moved quickly toward his truck. *I got to get out of here,* he thought. *What the hell just happened?* He leaned on the truck door and took several deep breaths, then turned the key and entered He put the coffee cup in the holder, laid the pastry on the dashboard and glanced at the clock; 4:32 p.m. Bob started the engine, and without a look back, drove onto the main street. In a couple of minutes he entered the traffic flow on I-39 headed through Rockford, north to pick up I-90 heading west into Wisconsin.

Scenes from the diner flashed through his mind. It was one of the most bizarre events that had ever happened to him, he mused. *What an asshole, that fat pig.* There could be trouble when Vinny woke up, maybe send the cops for him. No doubt, someone would remember the camper. He gulped: the comment about Montana; would Louise remember that and tell someone? He nervously looked at his mirrors but saw no police cruisers behind him.

Bob reached for his coffee; it was hot and tasted good. The pastry would have to hold him until he reached a campsite and prepared some supper. He tore the paper wrapper with his teeth and bit into the dough. Again he glanced at the mirror. No one behind him.

Bob let out a long breath. "Gotta put some miles between me and that diner," he mumbled. "Crissake, what an asshole."

He wondered if anyone in the diner had paid much attention to him, would recall what he looked like. The older couple had left and there had been only the group of self-engrossed teenagers. He checked the rear view mirror often. Slowly he calmed down from the adrenaline rush. He enjoyed the coffee and turned on the radio hunting for a local news station. There hadn't been any mention yet of the Lawndale Diner on the CB.

Why had he reacted like he did at the diner, he wondered? It had been so out of character, he mused, and so risky. As these thoughts went through his mind, he remembered scenes of his childhood, of his father beating his mother, of the fear and pain that she had suffered, and he knew that he couldn't have reacted any different. Vinny was just like his own father, always beating up on his mother. *What an asshole.* But he was glad that, at least, he didn't kill the guy. *Poor Louise, she'll have her hands full when that jerk wakes up. Lillian! What happened to her? She ran out of the place, but where?* He hoped that she would be safe from the brute. Her image played in his mind. An attractive woman, he thought, but there had been something else, something that had made him want to know her. He drove on into the evening.

—

Vinny struggled to get up, but then settled against the counter, vision blurred. He pulled his hand up against his aching head, trying to gather his senses. What had happened? He looked around but there was no one in the kitchen. Food and debris lay scattered on the floor. He balanced himself for another try at standing. His hand was red with his blood. Shaking his head, he tried to remember what had occurred. It slowly came back to him. *Who the hell hit me? Where is everybody? Where is that goddamn bitch?*

He stood up, holding on to the countertop, his head swimming. The pounding was worse standing up. He resisted the temptation to sit back down. Anger boiled up in him.

"Lillian!" he roared. No response. "Lillian!" he bellowed.

Louise appeared at the entrance to the kitchen. "Vinny...Vinny, you okay?"

"What happened...?"

"Guy heard you yelling and came back here...conked you on the head with a bottle."

"What guy? Where the hell is he?" he roared at her. She backed up from him.

"He...he left a few minutes ago. He got into a maroon truck...had a camper."

"Where'd he go? Which direction?" he roared.

"Saw him head toward the Interstate. Said something about Montana." Louise shook her head. "Vinny, you gotta help me. I hafta make some hamburgers and fries...customers out there." Louise went to the work table and started to put the food order together. "Vinny, please...help me with these orders."

"Goddamn bitch! Where the hell is she?" Vinny ignored the pleas for help.

"I don't know. I was out front. Maybe she's upstairs."

The rage only made his head hurt worse. He clenched his head between his hands and tried to calm himself. He would find her; fix that prissy bitch's face. He turned to the back stairs. "Hiding up there, are you?" he growled.

He slowly climbed the stairs, gripping the banister. His vision blurred again, his head pounded. At the top, he paused. He looked into his office, empty, and then he turned toward her room. The door was ajar. She was not there. He went to the window, looked down at the back parking area. *Her car is still there. Where is she? Where's the kid, what's his name? Jimmy.* He recalled now the a guy had come into the kitchen. *Crazy bastard…son of a bitch. Some goddamn Robin Hood.* He went to her closet and pulled open the door.

"Son of a bitch!" he roared. The closet was nearly empty. Her big tote bag was gone. He pulled open the drawers on the small dresser. They were empty.

"Bitch! I should have killed her… shoulda never hired her! Goddamn, Joey!" He turned toward the doorway, resting there a moment. He shook his head, tried to focus. He turned toward his office.

"Oh, shit!" His heart beat rapidly. Why hadn't he locked the door? He dropped into the desk chair. The computer was off; that was okay. But all the stuff on his desk had been shuffled. Vinny ran his hand over his brow. He was sweating, his head was killing him. What had she taken? So stupid to leave the door unlocked. He usually didn't. In a sudden realization, he turned in his chair to look toward his safe. The door was hanging open, but then he rarely locked it since he always locked the door to the office, but not this morning.

He got up from his chair, leaned on the safe, and pulled open the door.

"Oh, Christ!" Beads of sweat formed on his brow.

He started to shake. There had been three bags, one with cash, in the safe along with a pile of papers, now there were only two. "Oh, shit, shit, shit…"

He opened the first bag, rolls of coins and banded bills. He reached his hand under the cash and felt only the bottom of the cloth bag. His heart was pounding, his head throbbed. He reached for the second bag, pulled open the zipper, and reached under the cash and bills. He felt only the bottom of the bag. Panic seized him. He reached again into the bags, but it was useless. The third bag, the one with only banded bills, but with his CD and record book was gone - the CD with all the business files. He never stored anything important on the computer, since any smart ass could get into it, he had thought, especially any jackass with a search warrant. Everything was on the CD.

He tried to still his shaking hands and legs. He felt nauseous. Everything that he and Joey were involved in was recorded on that CD, and the record book held all the accounts. He had to find her. He would kill her, but first he had to get back the CD and the record book. He had to retrieve it before she gave the information to anyone, to the FBI.

"Joey, this is Vinny."

"Yeah, like I don't know your voice? What, you call maybe four – five times a day? What is it now?"

"Christ, Joey, we're in deep shit."

"What? What'd you do?" Joey sounded guarded.

"It was Lillian. She took a bag with bills. It was the one where I hid my CD and the record book, took it outa my safe."

"What? Where is she?"

"She's gone, can't find her. We had a fight. Some guy hit me. But . . . she . . . she's . . . gone. Vinny's voice betrayed his fear.

"What the hell you talking? Start at the fucking beginning!"

He related the story. Joey, didn't say a word, but Vinny could sense the rage. His hands trembled, the phone shook against his head.

"Joey, my head is bleeding…"

"Shut up! Where could she go? Where's Louise? Where's the kid, the dishwasher?" Vinny heard the anger in Joey's voice.

"Louise is here, working the customers, fixing orders. I don't know where Lillian went…not here. The kid's not here either. Her car is still out there."

"What'd Louise say?"

"She didn't see what happened…says, she was out front. She saw the guy drive off in a camper."

"You left the Goddamn safe open? Your office was open? What the hell is wrong with you?"

"Joey, I...I...I always lock my office...I don't know why I left it open. I...I," stuttered Vinny.

"Shut the hell up! This is goddamn serious. Where the hell could she go? Call the kid and find out where she went. What about this guy, who was he?"

"I don't know, a customer I guess. I was fixing a Salisbury steak at the time, must a been his."

"Who gives a shit about a goddamn steak? Where the hell is *she*? We *got* to get the CD and the book back right away! Damn it Vinny, you hearin' me?" Vinny knew that Joey was at the edge.

"Joey, I need your help. I can't think straight. Please," Vinny pleaded.

"You fuckin' asshole. I'm coming right over. You and Louise keep those customers happy. Don't leave the place and for Christ sake, don't put none of that shit up your nose."

Vinny heard the phone slam down as he jumped, his heart racing. He went downstairs into the kitchen. There was a Salisbury steak dinner to clean up.

Vinny sat bolt upright in his chair when he heard the pounding on the back door. Through the peephole, he saw Joey standing at the stoop. He unbolted the door.

"For Christ sake! How did this happen?" Joey exclaimed, his face red with anger and frustration as he pushed his way in past Vinny. "Did you call the kid? Does he know where she is?"

"I called him. Said he quit, ain't coming back here."

"No shit! Who cares? What did he say about Lillian? Where is *she*?" Joey's voice had a dangerous edge to it that made Vinny nervous.

"He said that he saw her leave by this back door. He doesn't know where she went. Said, she had her bags with her. I guess I was out cold at the time. The old bastard hit me with a bottle."

"You're going to get worse than that; you don't get that CD and book back."

Vinny closed his eyes and nodded.

"You dumb shit, she coulda gone with that old guy. He was back here in the kitchen when she left, right?"

"Yeah, that's what the kid said. She went out the back door. The old guy must have left after the kid."

Vinny knew they had to get the CD and the book back. It was imperative to their continued good health. She would die. He would see to that personally.

Joey's eyes bored into Vinny. "Let's say that somehow she left with the guy. Who we got out there we can send after her? I want that stuff back quick, and she has to be silenced. This is the last straw."

Vinny scratched his chin slowly. "There's Lou and Angelo, got them cooling their heels over to the Green Velvet pool hall. You know the place."

"Yeah? So what can they do for us? I don't want a couple of stumble bums, not for this." Joey looked at Vinny, a cold steely stare.

"Angelo is older, done some good clean work for me. Lou is a cowboy, but Angelo keeps him in line. I got them cooling it for a while. They cleaned out those apartments last week, all those jewels." Vinny rubbed his head. It was throbbing steadily.

"Yeah, that *was* good work. Okay, get them over here. Send them west bound on I-90."

"Sure Joey. I'll call them right now."

"Where's Ben and his side kick, Ernie?"

"I think they're at the warehouse."

"Find them. I want to send them east bound. Just in case."

"I'll get right on it."

———

Bob turned on the headlights when he crossed into Wisconsin. The sun had set. He studied the billboards carefully, hoping to find a campground before it got much darker. He was glad there was no mention of the Lawndale Diner in the CB chatter or on local radio. His nervousness had abated and he concentrated on looking for campground signs. A few miles before the Janesville turnoff, he saw a sign for Gary's Campground, less than a mile from I-90 on a rural road.

He pulled-into the campground and stopped at the office to register. With receipt and map in hand, he went back to the truck and drove to the assigned spot. He carefully pulled in so that he was close to the electric and water outlets. He gave a sigh of relief as he turned off the motor. It would be good to get to bed early, he thought. *What a crazy day.*

He removed an electric cable and a water hose from a compartment at the back of the camper and connected them to the campground facilities. Then he looked around the campground until he spotted the bathrooms, a short walk away. The campground was about half-full, a few truck campers, but mostly large motor homes. *I bet they are comfortable, but I'd hate to have to pay their fuel bill,* he mused. Darkness was upon them, lights were on in the motor homes, and some people were preparing supper on outside grills. He suddenly felt hungry.

Bob reached up to open the door to the camper, but the door handle wouldn't turn. *Huh? Did I lock it? Didn't think I did.* He reached into his pocket for his key ring. He slipped the key into the door lock and turned the handle. The door opened. A frightened looking woman was backed against the front of the camper, against the cab-over bed. Bob stood for a moment, speechless, mouth ajar. He recognized Lillian, still in her pink uniform, but he just stared.

"Please, I didn't have anywhere to go. Please," she pleaded.

"Lillian! What on earth are you doing here?" Bob said, incredulous.

"Please. I…It wouldn't start." She cowered against the back of the camper. "I didn't know where else to go."

"It's okay. Lillian. My name is Bob. Don't be afraid. It's okay." Bob tried to sound reassuring. His heart pounded.

"I was just so afraid. My car battery died. I panicked and just hid in here."

"It's okay. Don't be scared. Why don't you sit down here at the table?"

Lillian slid tentatively into the booth seat "I don't know what's going to happen. They'll come after me." Her voice trembled. Tears filled her eyes.

"You're okay for now. Here let me close the door. Will that be okay?" He reached for the doorknob.

She nodded, then pulled a tissue from her purse and wiped her eyes. She nervously wrapped and rewrapped the tissue, and clasped and intertwined her fingers.

"Who's going to come after you? Why?" Bob sat at the other end of the booth and rested his arms on the table.

Lillian shook her head and again wiped her eyes with the tissue. "Thank you for helping me." She looked down at her hands, her voice just above a whisper.

"I couldn't let him keep hitting you. I heard it out at the counter."

"What happened to him...to Vinny?" She stared at her hands.

"I knocked him out. He was okay when I left, breathing and all. He'll wake up with a real headache. I told Jimmy that he should go look for another job. He left right then."

"Jimmy is a good boy. Vinny, he...he's a brute. She looked up at him. "He *will* come after me to kill me."

"Why? Why will he come after you?"

Bob looked at her; again saw the fear in her eyes. She didn't say anything, just wrung her hands nervously.

"It'll be okay. Tell me." Her eyes welled up again.

She shook her head. "I'm really scared. Vinny, he's a mob guy and cousin to Joey DiCosta." She hesitated.

Bob nodded.

"Joey is my ex-husband. I agreed to go stay at Vinny's diner until I could get on my feet. Joey made me agree before he would let me leave him. He's so paranoid...wanted Vinny to watch me, afraid I would talk to the FBI. I wondered how come they hadn't killed me when I went for a divorce. I think that maybe Joey's boss didn't approve it." She stifled a sob. "They'll kill me now. I'm sure they will."

Fear distorted her face. Her lips trembled.

"Why? Why would they come after you?"

"They threatened before, that they would kill me if I talked about them to anyone. I...I took one of the bags from the safe upstairs. I only wanted some money, but when I looked inside of it just now, I found a CD and a record book. I know its Vinny's CD where he stores everything. He doesn't leave anything on his computer. And, I've seen the record book before. It's got all his accounts listed. Everything is in there. Oh God, when he sees that it's missing, he'll go insane. He'll tell Joey. They're both bad people. They're crazy."

"Lillian, you're away from them. You're okay now." He tried to sound reassuring.

"I shouldn't have taken those things. Oh God," she moaned and wiped her eyes. "Oh, please. Can you take me to the Greyhound station in Minneapolis?" she implored.

"Greyhound?"

"Yes, I can go to Atlanta or Ft. Lauderdale. I think people I know there would help me."

Bob didn't think she even believed what she was saying. She was like a frightened deer running from a hunter. "Sure, I can drop you off there tomorrow. You say you have money?"

"Yes, yes. In the bag I took."

Bob stood up. "Lillian, I have to fix myself something to eat. I never got my Salisbury Steak," he said with a wry grin.

"I'm sorry." She looked down at her hands.

"Forget it. I was just kidding. I'm going to make some hamburgers. Would you eat something?" He smiled.

She looked up at him and then nodded. "Yes, thank you." She fell silent.

———

They sat in the Monte Carlo, Angelo thumbing the roll of bills that Joey had given him. "Little over a grand," he mumbled. He looked over at Lou, slouched against the door. "Don't look so excited."

"What? How we gonna find those two? We'll have to go to hell and back." Lou cracked his knuckles.

"We *have* to find them, you heard the man. Get that road atlas outa the back seat."

"What about Ben and Ernie? They're going east."

"Waste of time. Get your head in that atlas," said Angelo.

Angelo didn't like the kid much. Gutsy, a real wild card. They had done well on the jewelry robbery; a well planned operation. Lou had managed to stay focused and they had made a rapid sweep through the expansive condo. The haul had to be worth a couple of million, he pondered. This was his bag, he thought, not chasing some dame and an old fart across the country. What would he have to do then, kill them? He wasn't a killer, although he would if it meant getting caught otherwise. One stint in prison had been enough. He wasn't going back, not for anyone. Well, he'd do his best to find them.

"They have a couple hours head start on us," said Angelo. "Louise at the diner told Vinny that he had seen this guy get into a truck camper with a Mass. plate. He told her that he was headed toward Montana. Said, he seemed to be some retired geezer."

"If she's in that camper with this dude, then they're probably on the Interstate." Lou was looking at the Illinois map.

"Wow, that's brilliant," exclaimed Angelo.

"Most likely on I-90," said Lou, his fingers tracing the routes on the map. "Coulda taken her into Chicago too, I guess."

"Chicago? During rush hour? What the hell for? Hey, this guy doesn't know anything about the dame, probably just giving her a ride outa here. He's a vacationer, probably headed for the national parks, maybe visiting relatives. Christ, he's in a *camper*." Angelo shook his head. "Look, we're losing time. He's got maybe two hours head start if he kept going. I'm heading west on I-90. We'll check all the campgrounds out that way. He won't be driving all night; he probably was behind the wheel all day already."

"Okay. You're the boss," Lou conceded. He dropped the road atlas on the floor.

Angelo started the car. The powerful modified engine rumbled to life. They left the back of the diner and made a left to get to I-39 northbound. On the highway, the speedometer moved quickly to 80.

"Lou, when we get clear of this area start looking for campground signs, any kind of campground. We'll check 'em all."

"Yeah, sure. He could be over a hundred miles in front of us."

"Maybe, or he could be in a campground already. Keep your goddamn eyes open. We fail in this, Joey won't take it easy on us."

The sun set as they left Rockford behind. Suddenly, Lou pointed to a small sign, *Richardson's RV camping, next exit*. At the exit they saw another sign, *Camping, left, 0.8 miles*. He made a left and stopped before the campground entrance.

"I'm going to cruise through slowly. You watch for truck campers. We'll check them out." Angelo drove through the park slowly.

"Mostly RV units. Oh, there, ahead. That's a truck camper. There's another just past it." Lou peered into the darkness. "Yeah, there's a third one...a maroon truck."

"Keep your eyes open. I'm going to stop on the other side of this loop for a couple minutes, see who comes and goes."

"Ain't none of 'em with Mass. plates," commented Lou.

"I'll stop here for a few minutes; maybe Louise made a mistake on the plates."

He drove past the three truck campers and turned in the loop drive so that they could see all three of them. He turned off his lights, but left the engine running. In a few minutes he started back out of the park. All three campers had young couples and children, not what they were looking for. Back on the highway, they headed north. The speedometer crept past 80.

"Hey, look." Lou gestured toward a sign just coming into clear view. "There, Gary's Campground. Take the next exit, 0.9 of a mile on the right."

"Okay. That's the Janesville exit," Angelo said.

CHAPTER 5 NO TURNING BACK

Bob picked up her big bag and put it on the bunk and then tossed up the smaller one. Reaching up, he opened the vent a bit and then cracked open the window. From the refrigerator, he removed a package of hamburger meat and busied himself at the sink.

"Bob, I'm sorry I got you into this. I'll get out of your hair when you drop me off at the bus station. It's me they'll be looking for."

"Don't worry about *me*. Relax for a while. There's time to think about it."

Soon he had a pot of mixed vegetables cooking on the stove-top as he prepared the hamburgers in a frying pan. After placing it on the burner, Bob readied his coffee maker.

"Lillian, would you mind fixing the table? There's a tablecloth in the cupboard above you and silverware in the drawer next to the fridge."

She got up. "Sure, really happy to do something." She spread the tablecloth and took silverware from the drawer. "Do you have napkins?"

He turned toward her and smiled. With a nod, he indicated the cupboard above her head. "They're in there somewhere."

She looked into his eyes and then smiled at him. "I should be doing that."

"No, sit down, relax. It'll just be a few more minutes." He turned back to tend to his cooking.

"I'll be out of your hair tomorrow. I promise."

"You're okay for now. I don't mind you being here. Truly, I don't."

"You're too kind," she said in almost a whisper.

Lillian was quiet as Bob put servings of mixed vegetables, hamburger and bread on two porcelain camp plates. He set them at the place settings and sat down facing her.

"It's not the Ritz, but it should take care of the hunger. Drink? I have coffee just made, or would you rather have water?" He went to the coffee maker.

"Thank you for this. Appreciate it. I'll have coffee, too." She looked up at him and smiled.

God, I love that voice. He took another cup out of the cupboard, and put the non-dairy creamer on the table. "Sorry, I don't have any real cream. It doesn't keep well."

"Fake cream is fine, thanks. I don't know what all you put in the hamburger, but it sure is good, and it's juicy too."

"Just an old recipe of mine."

"I like it."

"Thanks. Enough? More bread?" He looked at her.

She looked up. "I'm fine. Coffee's good."

"Tell me, what kind of trouble did you have back there with this Vinny guy?"

She hesitated for some seconds. "I thought that Joey would kill me when I wanted to leave him. He thought that I would go to the FBI...but I wouldn't." She paused again. "Finally I agreed... to stay at the diner and open mornings for Vinny. I thought that that would work, but I didn't know Vinny well."

"Louise and Jimmy said he hit you."

She nodded, "He's such a pig, a disgusting and evil man. And he snorts all the time...makes him crazy."

"Damn. It sounds like you really stepped into it." Bob shook his head.

"I was young when I married Joey. A mob guy - it was so exciting then, and there was always money for anything."

"Didn't last, I guess," prompted Bob.

She shook her head. "Gradually, he stayed away from home more and more. He didn't take me to very many places after a while. He didn't want a family...made that clear. That was a real disappointment for me."

"No children..."

"No...that hurt my parents, too." She paused. "Then there were all the other women. He never bothered to deny it, just said that was the way it was. He and Vinny own these clubs and liquor stores, as well as the diner and truck place behind it. There's always something going on he won't talk to me about. People disappearing, shootings, extortion, and I'm sure they're even skimming from the boss.

"Skimming? I'm surprised those two aren't dead already."

"I guess they bring in enough money, and no one knows about the skimming. I only know because I overheard him and Vinny talking about it."

"How long were you with him?" asked Bob.

"I married him when I was nineteen…had stars in my eyes. I left him finally three years ago after eighteen years. He fought the divorce; told me that if I talked to the FBI, he would have me killed. I believed him then… still do."

"Long time."

"The priest kept talking me into staying and working it out. I think Joey put pressure on him."

Bob shook his head. "I should have hit the bastard harder."

"I'm sorry I got you into this." Lillian looked as if she was going to cry again.

"I'm just glad I was there. I heard about the diner on the CB from a couple of truckers."

"Yeah, the place has a rep for big servings that won't make you sick. They also have a bunch of guys who bring in stolen goods. That warehouse is full of stuff."

"Sitting there…I was wondering what Vinny was doing to you. I mean, you definitely brightened up the place."

She answered easily, looking into his eyes for a moment. "The work in the diner was okay. I didn't make much. We were losing customers to a new Denny's near the Interstate."

"Yeah, I saw the place when I came into town."

"The bastard wouldn't keep his hands off me, even in front of Jimmy. What a pig. He and Joey started to put pressure on me to work at their clubs to do stripping, fill-in between the featured dancers. They kept offering me a lot of money and then started threatening me, suggesting that they would spread rumors about me talking to the FBI. I have *never* talked to FBI or to any law people, for that matter. They've come up to me in stores and in parking lots, trying to get me to sit down with them. I never did and I never will. I've seen what happens to those that do."

Bob met her gaze. "No one should have to live like that."

"I was so angry when I left there. I didn't use common sense. I just wanted to hurt him. Taking that bag of money with the CD and his record book - it's going to get me killed. I didn't know it was in there, I just wanted some money. I know that he and Joey will be looking to get those things back and to make me pay. They'll kill me. I'm sorry Bob. Sorry I got you into this." Tears wet her face. She clasped her trembling hands together.

Bob put a hand over her clasped fingers. She looked up at him.

"Lillian, don't think about it now. Tomorrow we can talk about what you can do."

"I'm frightened."

"I know." Bob reached for the coffee carafe and refilled both their cups again. "Want something in it? Got some Jim Beam in the cupboard."

She shook her head and smiled, "I'm fine. Thanks."

Bob saw the two men when he left the men's room with his toiletries. They stood blocking the path back to the camper. The men's room door slammed shut again behind him, and he could hear boisterous voices in jocular friendship off to his left. Bob started to move around the two men on the pathway, trying to ignore their presence.

"Hey, pal, you're the fellow that stopped at the Lawndale Diner back in Illinois. Yeah, we got a description from a guy next door at the warehouse."

He was the older of the two. The other one had an insolent smirk on his face. Bob looked squarely at both of them, wrinkled his face in feigned confusion, and replied. "Yeah, big deal. What? I didn't leave enough freaking tip?"

"Hey, fella, let's make this easy," said the older man. "Where's the woman, the waitress, Lillian?"

The silent one still had the smirk on his face.

"How would I know? When I left she was standing against the building. A black Pontiac pulled up and she got in. I didn't pay much attention."

The older one shook his head. "That's not what the witness at the warehouse says." The man gave him a hard look. The younger one just smirked.

"Screw your witness. Maybe you better check his eyesight. He couldn't have seen the front of the diner from the warehouse. Good night." Bob started walking. The one with the smirk moved to block his way. Bob felt heat creep up his neck.

"You got a problem?" asked Bob as he pulled out his cell phone. He popped open the cover. "I should call 911, let them sort it out."

The older man tugged on Lou's sleeve. They turned and strode toward the front of the campground heading toward a dark colored car parked near the entryway; *a late model Monte Carlo*, Bob thought, but wasn't sure.

—

"Angelo, she's probably in the damn camper! We could've got her!"

"What? Pop the guy there in front of everybody? Are you nuts? Just cool it. I'm gonna call Vinny." *Goddamn loose cannon, always looking for trouble. I'm getting too old for this shit.* Angelo pulled his cell phone from his jacket pocket and punched in Vinny's number.

"Yeah, it's me, boss."

"Did you find them?" Vinny asked.

"We found the camper in an RV park. We just now braced the driver. He claims she left in a black Pontiac. He got real porky when we pressed him and told him we didn't believe him. He pulled out his cell phone and said he was going to call the cops. We backed off. There were too many people around to make him eat his phone. So we came back to the car to call you."

"So you don't know where she is? She could be right there in the damn camper!"

"We didn't want to create a scene, boss. There's lots of people around." His excuse sounded lame, now that he said it out loud.

"Listen, damn it!" Angelo pulled the phone away from his ear. "You two guys find a place to park where you can see if anyone comes out of the campground. One of you better be awake at all times. They leave, follow them, you know what to do! Is that understood?"

"Sure, boss. That's what we're gonna do."

"Get me that stuff! Do as we planned and I want it done quick! You hearin' me?" Vinny yelled into the phone.

"We got it, boss."

Angelo heard a click and closed his cell phone, putting it back in his pocket. He wiped his brow with the back of his hand and looked over at Lou.

"He ain't too damn happy."

"We should've popped the prick, and then the woman in the camper. She's in there, I'm sure."

"Yeah, smart guy. And then what? Send the stuff back to Vinny UPS from a jail cell?"

Lou smirked at Angelo and shook his head. "Shoulda popped him."

"Shut up. I gotta find a place to park where we can keep an eye on the entrance here."

"Just terrific…sleep all night in the goddamn car…terrific." Lou scowled at Angelo.

Bob went back to the camper, climbed in and closed the door. He pushed the lock button.

"What?" Lillian looked at him with apprehension. She was sitting at the table with her coffee.

"A couple of characters stopped me out there when I came out of the men's room."

"No!" Lillian turned white, her eyes wide. "Oh God!"

"They're gone now, but I'm sure we'll see them again tomorrow." Bob spoke softly, hoping not to panic her.

"What? What did they want?" she gasped.

"They claimed that they had a witness at the warehouse that saw me leave the diner in the camper. Apparently, this witness had not seen you. They're assuming that you left with me. I told them that you left after I did by the front door and got into a black Pontiac. I don't think that they believed me, though. I pulled out my cell phone, threatened to call the cops. They went back to their car. Probably calling for instructions."

"Oh God, they found me." Tears welled in her eyes and her hands trembled. She clasped the cup in both hands to still them.

"Should you give the bag back to these guys?" asked Bob.

She shook her head. "They'll still come after me. I know too much. It was okay while I was at the diner."

"Lillian, we're okay here for now. We'll figure something out tomorrow."

"I brought you into this. Now they'll hurt you, too." She wiped at her eyes with her hand.

Bob sat down at the table and placed both of his hands on hers. "You're okay now. They're gone. We'll figure out what to do tomorrow."

She looked into his eyes. Tears rolled down her face.

Bob stood outside the restrooms while Lillian went inside. He peered into the darkness, but didn't see anything suspicious. He looked carefully about the campground for any movement. All was still. He had to think of how to get away from these thugs. Likely those two would get to them in the morning. What could he do? Think; he had to think. He saw Lillian leave the building. She looked at him anxiously.

"It's okay. All's quiet," said Bob.

She hurried to the camper and he locked the door when they were inside.

He pointed to the cab-over bunk. "Listen, the bunk has a curtain that you can draw across it, see? You go on and take the bunk; I'll fix myself a place down here. This table and seat breaks down into a bed."

"I can't take your bed. Your sleeping bag is up there. I'll stay down here." She looked at him, her face reddened.

"No, I want to stay by the door. I'll be fine. I have blankets in the cupboard. You go on, use the sleeping bag. There's no bed bugs." He grinned, trying to lighten the awkward moment.

"That's so nice of you. I have no right to do this."

"It's fine, I want to be by the door. Oh, by the way. There is an emergency chemical toilet right in front of the closet. The step-up to the bunk lifts and it's underneath. If you really need to use it, you can draw the curtain next to it." He pointed out the curtain and showed her how the toilet was set up.

"I hope I won't need it." She forced a smile.

"I'll step out for a few minutes and you can get ready for bed. I'll take a walk around, see the layout of the place."

"Be careful."

He nodded and left the camper, standing still for a minute letting his eyes get accustomed to the dark. There were small lights everywhere, windows of campers and trailers and some large RV units. He could just make out the large units parked at the rear of the campground. Was there another way out? He walked casually down the road, his eyes scanning the darkness. As he passed the RV units, he saw several large dumpsters in a row. Turning, he spotted a narrow road heading into the trees. The road was deeply rutted from heavy traffic; the trash trucks, he thought. It had to be a back way into town. He recalled from the map, that US-14 went close by, a back way to get to Madison. The thugs would likely be looking for them on I-90 when they didn't appear at the front entrance in the morning. Well, he would slip out early, out the back way.

Inside, he prepared the dinette into a bed. Lillian had her curtain drawn. Bob stayed in his jeans, not wanting to be at too much of a disadvantage if he were to get company. It was a while before he fell asleep.

—

Angelo checked his watch then looked over at Lou. "Are you awake?"

"Huh? Yeah," responded Lou. "Anything happening?"

"If you stayed awake, you'd know."

"Christ…just let me slip into the campground. I'll get them to come out of the damn camper…watch me." Lou tried to get comfortable, bunching his jacket under his head.

"What? Knock on the door? Maybe he has a gun in there, think of that?"

Lou didn't open his eyes. "Screw it. You want Vinny climbing down your throat? Fine. Do what you want."

"What I want is not to get caught and end up back in prison."

"Yeah, yeah."

CHAPTER 6 FEAR, VIOLENCE AND FRIENDS

Bob woke before five and lay in his bed going over all that had happened the past day, wondering what he could do to help Lillian without getting himself killed. He liked her.

A few minutes later, Bob took his toiletries and towel into the men's room, making sure to lock the camper door. He relaxed under the hot shower for a few minutes. Shaved and with clean clothes, he went back to the camper. The door opened as he got there and Lillian appeared, somewhat apprehensively stepping onto the ground.

"I didn't know where you had gone…" she started.

"I was just going to wake you. I think maybe we can give those jerks the slip if we leave soon. There's a back way out of here for utility trucks. I'm gambling that we can get to US-14 and get into Madison without their knowing it. We can pick up I-90 again in Madison."

"Okay, I'll get ready real quick. It'll be just a few minutes. I promise."

Bob went into the camper and started to put things away for traveling. He tore down the bed and set up the dinette table and cushions; then tossed his bags on the bunk with Lillian's. Outside, he shut off the LPG tank and disconnected the service hookups. The cable and hoses went into the storage compartment.

Lillian was back in a few minutes, looking about nervously. "No make up - hope I don't scare you."

"Quite lovely," said Bob giving her an appreciative glance.

"Thank you." She squeezed his arm and climbed into the camper.

Her touch pleased him.

"Should I sit back here? They won't see me." She looked at Bob, uncertain.

"Yes, that would be best…at least until we get to Madison. If they see the truck with just me in it, they may think you went your own way."

"Okay."

"There's the little pass-through window if you want to tell me something."

She nodded and looked at him frowning.

"We'll be okay," he said.

They went slowly out of the campground, following the utility road through the trees until it came out on a local street. Bob turned away from the campground and was soon in an area of storage buildings, truck repair facilities, and fuel storage tanks. He saw the sign for US-14 and turned onto another local street. Shortly he turned again onto US-14. It was getting light as he headed north from Janesville.

They reached the outskirts of Madison in less than an hour, and Bob pulled into a small service station, stopping at the fuel pumps.

"I'll fill up here. It's kinda out of the way," said Bob, turning his head towards the pass-thru window. "I saw a McDonalds down the street, maybe we can hide the camper in back and get some breakfast."

"That would be nice," replied Lillian.

As he got out of the truck, he looked around but saw only early morning traffic on the street. No one was parked nearby. He cleaned off the windshield, picked up his credit card receipt from the pump, and then drove the short distance to McDonalds. He looked around again, and didn't see the Monte Carlo. He knocked on the camper door and Lillian climbed down to the ground. There was a hint of color on her cheeks and a touch of lipstick. Bob smiled.

—

"Wake up, goddamn it. Wake up!" Angelo looked at his watch, 6:08. He rubbed his eyes. The sky was getting light. "Oh, shit. Both of us asleep."

Lou stirred and shifted his body against the window.

"Wake the hell up! It's daylight!" A tinge of panic rippled through Angelo. He looked toward the entrance of the trailer court. Everything seemed quiet. The tourists would be pouring out of there soon, back to the highway.

"Get your ass down to the campground, see what's happening."

"All right…but I need some coffee." Lou ran his fingers through his hair and straightened his rumpled clothes.

"Check out the campground and *then* we'll think about coffee and something to eat."

Lou got out of the car, put on his jacket, and started toward the campground.

———

They sipped coffee with their Egg McMuffin. Lillian looked out of the window, and scrutinized each car and person that passed by.

"They'll be waiting for us somewhere." Lillian glanced up at his face.

Bob nodded. "I'm pretty sure they're out there."

"Bob, drop me off at the bus station in Milwaukee. I'll take my chances and try to get somewhere safe. I have some friends in Atlanta and in Ft. Lauderdale." Lillian nervously fidgeted with her coffee cup.

"Lillian, you can't live like that. I mean, for how long? It sounds like these guys are a little nuts and maybe a little desperate for their own survival."

"Please. I can't do this to you. It isn't fair. You've helped me so much already. I can't bring them down on you, too." Her eyes glistened.

"You want to just drop in on your friends? They don't know you're coming. They maybe don't want the complication. You need to know. You need to call them." Bob was touched by the sadness on her face.

"I *should* call them," her voice was strained.

"Can you give back the stuff you took? Would that get them off your back?" asked Bob.

She shook her head. "They'll want to get the CD and record book, sure. But then they'll kill me to shut me up. Vinny and Joey are afraid of what I know, of what I can tell about their skimming. If anyone found out about it, about their offshore accounts, the crew boss, Frank Cappella, would have those two in a landfill by nightfall." She shook her head. "Vinny is such a terrible person. He'd kill me just for running out on him. And now, they probably think I've looked at the stuff on the CD." She wiped the tears from her face with her napkin.

Bob met her gaze. "I don't know where I'm going really. My first stop will be to visit my cousin on a guest ranch on the Idaho-Montana border. I'll stay there a little while if I can. Beyond that I haven't made any plans. I want to write and I'll probably do that in different places." He rubbed his chin. "Anyway, what I want to say is you're welcome to come with me. You've got no place to go either. It would all be on the up-and-up, you won't have to be afraid of me."

She looked calmly into his eyes. "I'm not afraid of you. You're a good man. I know that. I can't bring this trouble upon you." Her eyes seemed to reach into him. He wanted to touch her face.

"I'd like it if you would let me help you. Of course, you can always decide to take a bus or a plane. But let me help you until then."

Tears ran down her face. She looked at him silently.

"Come with me. Let me help you."

"Okay." It was barely a whisper.

—

Angelo looked up and saw Lou running toward him. His breath caught in his throat. "Oh shit!"

Lou opened the door. "They're gone! The son of a bitch is gone!" he gasped and collapsed into the seat. "I asked a couple getting set to leave if they had seen our friends take off. They hadn't but thought they heard an engine start around five or five thirty."

Angelo was already looking at the map. "They got an hour, maybe more, start on us. It's quarter past six."

"Vinny will be plenty pissed, he hears about this," Lou said.

"Yeah, we both dozed off. We got to find them." Angelo started the engine, made a U-turn, and sped down the local road. "Best bet is I-90. They probably think that they're rid of us."

"Find a drive-thru, got to get something to eat and some coffee," said Lou.

"Okay. Look for one before we get to I-90."

—

Wal-Mart in Madison was only a few minutes from opening as Bob and Lillian pulled into the parking lot. Lillian had mentioned her need for a change of clothes and to replace items she had left behind in her haste. Bob parked close to the store entrance, hoping to avoid trouble. He had an uneasy feeling as he looked around; sure he hadn't seen the last of the two goons. Twenty minutes later, Lillian put her purchases in the camper and they were on their way through Madison.

Bob checked the map again, and chose US-12, which ran parallel to I-90 until the I-94 interchange. Two hours later, Bob turned onto State Route-21 which stayed close to I-90 and would take them into La Crosse.

"This isn't the fastest way to anywhere, but I bet those jerks are speeding down I-90 wondering how we got so far ahead." Bob turned and grinned.

"Think we're okay?" asked Lillian.

"At some point, those guys will realize they've been had. I'm hoping they give up."

He saw the worry frown on her face.

"They'll find us…" she whispered.

———

Angelo pushed the car to 85. "How much of a lead do they have?" he muttered. He was sure they had sped off on I-90. After all, they didn't know the roads around here. The old guy was a tourist.

"Damn it. I could have popped them both last night," grumbled Lou with obvious disdain for Angelo's decision to hold back. "It'd be all over now. We'd be going home. When we going to get another chance, in goddamn Wyoming?" Lou shook his head. "Vinny is gonna go crazy when he hears this."

"It's my call," Angelo said with an edge to his voice. "Sure. Pop them where everyone can get a good view of us. What? You expect that we'd get outa there and no one would spot us, get our plates, and call 911? Holy shit, use your head." Angelo wished he had come alone. Then he added, "I ain't goin' back to prison."

"We're already past Madison. We staying on I-90, or would they go up I-94 into North Dakota?" Lou stared at the map.

"Hell do I know? I'm stayin' with I-90. What's in North Dakota, for crissake?"

Lou glanced at Angelo and scowled. "They can't be that far ahead. What? Maybe got an hour or so head start? That's 60 – 80 miles. We'll catch 'em before long." Lou tossed the map book on the floor.

—

Bob stayed at the speed limit along Route 21, and the miles drifted by as Bob and Lillian talked about their lives. He saw that Lillian glanced often at the rear view mirror.

"I'm sure they're on I-90 thinking they can catch up to us," said Bob.

She nodded. "They won't give up."

There were periods of several minutes when neither spoke. When Lillian did make conversation, it was about her childhood, growing up in a middle class family in Chicago. She had no siblings, but mentioned her parents were still alive.

She turned and smiled. "They still live in the same house I grew up in."

"That has to be comfortable for them. Where did your dad work?" asked Bob.

"He's a machinist…worked in several auto parts plants. He took good care of us."

"Your mom? She was at home?" asked Bob.

"Yes, during my childhood. She went to work after I got married. I think that was mainly to keep busy." She paused, gazing out the window.

Bob offered, "My mother worked in a print shop after I was a few years old. My dad worked in the garment mills until they closed and moved down south. Now the mills are not even in the US anymore. Afterward, my dad worked for the railroad. I did, too. We both were machinists."

"You're not 65, are you?" she asked, her eyes widening.

Bob grinned. "No, I'm 53…got downsized into retirement."

"You're divorced, huh?" she asked.

"Mmm," Bob nodded. "I have a son and a couple grandkids in Atlanta. I haven't seen them in a couple of years. He's in finance, doing okay."

"Your parents still alive?" she asked.

"No, both died a few years back."

They fell silent. Bob glanced at her a few times. He wondered how he could help her. He liked her, but there was something else, something he hadn't put into words - yet.

Bob started talking again. "After a while I just didn't feel like staying in Massachusetts any longer. It isn't like what I grew up with any more. Hardly recognize it."

"Times change…" she remarked, looking again into her rear view mirror. "When I met Joey, he just swept me off my feet. I guess the flash and money and socializing was more than I could resist. I married him a year later."

"Right out of high school?"

"Yep. My parents weren't too thrilled, but I was smitten," she said. "I wanted to go to college at night, make something out of myself, but Joey wouldn't hear of it. I soon learned of his dark side - a real control freak. I finally gave up trying to change his mind."

"I'm sorry…"

"He refused to have children. I guess that saddened me the most."

"You stayed with him."

"Yes, my parents, the priest…they wanted me to make it work. I tried, but he just wanted someone he could take places, and to be there when he wanted me." She looked down at her lap, fell silent for a minute. Bob glanced at her, saw the sadness on her face. She continued without looking up. "I gradually became aware of his womanizing and realized that it had been going on from the beginning. When I tried to get help from the priest, all I got was sympathy. I think now Joey was bribing him with large church donations."

Bob shook his head.

She glanced at him. "Then the FBI started to nose around. They tried to enlist me, coerce me into helping them. It terrified me. I knew what happened to people that went over…friends who suddenly disappeared. Some of Joey's boys probably saw me being approached by the FBI and told Joey. He hardly came home anymore, and when he did…"

"The witness protection program is no kind of life," Bob offered.

"Joey threatened me often. He said that no one had ever snitched on him and lived. That frightened me."

"How did you get a divorce? It must have been scary," asked Bob.

"During all that, I often thought that he would kill me. He terrorized me often, threats, breaking things, slapping me around. He worried most about my talking about what I knew, and he said if I did, he would have me hunted down and killed." She looked down at her lap, wringing her hands. "I believe him."

—

About 100 miles north of Madison, I-90 turned west and I-94 kept north for some distance before turning west toward Minneapolis. Angelo pulled off the road at a highway department gate just before the interchange.

"What are you doing? What's wrong?" asked Lou looking around as the car came to a stop.

"Look, they can't be ahead of us. As fast as we were going, we'da caught up with them before now. They musta stopped or are driving pretty damn slow. We'll wait here 'till they come by. They'll be easy enough to spot."

"Maybe they took a different road." Lou picked up the map book again.

"Damn unlikely. He's a tourist. He'll be on I-90. He's gotta be headin' this way. I guess there's always a slim chance he'd go straight ahead here onto I-94, although I can't imagine why. When we pick up his tail, we'll see." Angelo settled back in his seat.

"We don't get 'em soon, we never will. Vinny will take it out on us." He looked at Angelo. "You know he will."

"Yeah, I know."

—

Lillian noticed Bob looking at the rear-view mirrors often.

"Bob…is…are they back there?" Her face strained in worry.

"Don't think so. I hope they're far ahead of us by now."

Lillian didn't say anything. She looked into the rear view mirror on her side.

"I'm afraid," she said softly.

Bob reached over and took her hand and squeezed it, hoping to comfort her. She squeezed back hard, not looking at him.

They rode in silence for a while.

"You getting hungry?" Bob asked.

"A little. I wouldn't mind some coffee."

"Yeah. Me too," he replied. "There…there's a convenience store, and it has gas pumps."

He stopped in front of the pumps.

"I can run in and get coffee, see if they have a decent sandwich," said Lillian. "What kind do you like?"

"Ham and cheese would be good. Otherwise just pick one."

Lillian went into the store while Bob topped off the tank. She was back in the truck as Bob hung up the fuel nozzle.

"What'd you get?" asked Bob.

"You got a ham and cheese on wheat. I got a tuna salad."

"We're kind of exposed here, I should keep moving."

Lillian nodded, and handed Bob his sandwich.

When Bob looked into the mirrors a few minutes later, Lillian became alarmed.

"You were staring at a car. Is it them?" she asked.

"No. I wasn't sure for a few seconds. Local guy just pulled off."

Bob stayed at the speed limit, sipped his coffee and finished his sandwich. "Not much traffic on this road, everyone up on the Interstate."

"I hope *they* are," she said.

The Interstate appeared on their left from time to time as they drove through many small towns. It would have been an enjoyable ride, except for not knowing what would happen with the two thugs. Lillian asked him about his married life, his son, how it had all ended.

Bob grimaced. "We got married very young. We were both nineteen and it seemed like the thing to do. Our parents encouraged it; they'd been married early. I think they were more interested in grandkids. It wasn't long before our son came along."

"Joey didn't want kids."

"Actually, our son was an accident, but I was happy about it. I enjoyed raising him, even as a teenager."

"You and your wife were not much more than kids yourselves." Lillian said with a grin.

"I was terribly immature, probably why we had so many problems," Bob added.

Lillian glanced at him. "Most guys are at that age."

"I was very defensive, self centered, with an unwarranted ego. Pretty soon we both put up defenses against each other. We became more like brother and sister, and we eventually were in separate bedrooms."

"I'm sorry," she said. "So sad." She stared out the windshield and continued. "Joey wanted me there when he came home – whenever that was. Sometimes he'd be away for days at a time. After a while, I was hoping he'd never come back."

Bob shook his head.

"He had his boss, Santos, over one afternoon as well as the big man, Cappella. I don't remember the occasion anymore, but there were quite a few guys there. Joey was drinking heavy, and started hitting me about something. I remember Cappella said something to Santos. Santos took Joey outside and came back in without him. I didn't see Joey for several days."

"Pretty scary business, doing what those guys do."

"Joey's been arrested several times, but always got off. Witnesses disappear, things like that." She glanced at him, and then looked away as he turned to reply.

"Was he always in that line of work?"

"Uh-huh. At first, it was exciting and glamorous. There was money for whatever we wanted, parties, dining. I was so naïve. Unbelievable."

"You married right out of high school."

"Had stars in my eyes. Reality began to settle in after a year or so. I overheard more and more about the business he was in, saw the friends he had, saw that some disappeared suddenly. I became scared when he started to threaten me about talking to the FBI. The FBI was nosing around. His crew had found some bugs that had been planted in one of their meeting places back of a pizza shop."

"They tried to get to you?"

"Oh, yes. They approached me many times in parking lots and stores. Joey heard about it and was incensed. I never talked to the FBI, not ever."

"And he didn't kill you."

"I think he would have had to get an okay from Cappella."

—

The state patrol cruiser came to a quick stop along the shoulder of the highway. With blue lights flashing, the cruiser backed up and stopped in front of the Monte Carlo, blocking their way back to the travel lane.

"Oh shit!" exclaimed Lou. He pulled his pistol from under his jacket and stuffed it under the seat.

"Just relax. I'll talk to him," said Angelo. "Maybe he's pissed about my parking here."

The patrolman was still in his car, microphone held up to his face. Two minutes went by and then the patrolman left the car and looked down the highway into oncoming traffic. A half minute later another patrol car stopped. A few seconds of conversation, and the two patrolmen approached on each side of the Monte Carlo. Angelo lowered his window. Lou left his up.

"Good morning, gentlemen. What seems to be the trouble?" the officer asked of Angelo.

"The damn thing keeps heating up. Pulled over to let it cool," Angelo shrugged.

"Where you fellows headed?" he asked Angelo. Lou slouched casually in his seat, glancing toward Angelo occasionally, and ignoring the officer outside his door.

"We got friends in Sioux Falls; hoping to make it there and get the problem fixed," replied Angelo.

"Please hand me your driver's license and registration."

"Sure." he turned to Lou. "Get the registration outa the glove box." Angelo pulled his billfold from his jacket and took out the license. Lou passed him the registration.

"This is the entrance for a state highway maintenance facility," said the officer. "It can be a dangerous place to get off and back on the highway. You're going to have to move on."

Angelo met his glance and nodded.

"Be right back," said the officer and walked to his car. The other officer stood by the passenger door and waited.

"Of all the goddamn luck!" whispered Angelo. "Now they're running the plates and license. How long will that take?"

Lou took the opportunity to criticize Angelo, but kept his voice down. "We shouldn't have parked here. Only emergency parking is allowed on the Interstate. They'd be bound to check us out." Lou tried to look nonchalant and thumbed through the map book. He wasn't at all sure that the cops had bought the story of the car running hot, sitting here to let it cool off. He wondered if the outstanding warrants on him had made it into the NCIC data. He'd know soon enough.

"Keep your eyes peeled for the damn camper," mumbled Angelo.

"Yeah. Nothing to do now but wait until these cops get done screwing with their computer," whispered Lou.

"Keep your eyes open, they could be behind us. That old fart might be smarter than we give him credit for."

"We'll catch up with them...if they're ahead of us." Lou stared at the traffic.

"What the hell is taking so long?" Angelo stared at the patrolman in the cruiser.

"Here he comes."

The returning patrolmen stepped up to Angelo's window, handing him back his license and registration.

"I expect that you'll want to have the heating problem looked at. There is a Conoco station six miles up on I-90. I'll stay behind you, make sure you get there okay."

"Thank you officer, appreciate that." Angelo started the car and feigned concern by looking at the temperature gauge. A minute later one police cruiser had departed. The other waited with flashers on while Angelo merged into the traffic flow. [why would he back up. He might put on his directional signal and just wait for Angelo to work back into the traffic flow]

"I don't know what they're thinking. Something might have come up on the computer. We'll play along, go to the Conoco and wait until he takes off again," said Angelo.

"Yeah, he won't hang around there long."

The police cruiser stopped in front of the Conoco building, while Angelo parked the Monte Carlo alongside the service entrance.

"What we gonna do now?" asked Lou, turning to see where the policeman was.

"I'm gonna play along, what the hell else am I gonna do? I'll go in and ask the mechanic some dumb questions, stall for time until the cop goes away."

"He's probably late for his coffee and donuts," Lou laughed.

Angelo got out of the car and walked into the service bay where two men were working under the hood of a car. One fellow looked up on hearing Angelo clear his throat.

"You can't be in here, buddy…insurance."

"Sure. Sorry." Angelo started to back away. "I was wondering if you could check out my car. It's been over heating."

"Give me 15-20 minutes here, and then we'll take a look."

Angelo nodded and walked back out of the service bay.

The state trooper was leaning on his car and looked at him inquiringly. "They gonna take care of you?"

Angelo shrugged. "They said it'd be twenty minutes before they could look at it."

The trooper's attention suddenly shifted to the voice from his radio. He quickly got into his car. "Drive safe now, you hear?" The door closed and he sped away.

—

"We'll have to get back onto I-90, Bob. I don't see any parallel road we can take out of La Crosse." Lillian was studying the map.

"Okay. I don't want to meet them on one of these side roads. It'll be a bit safer on the Interstate." Bob glanced at her. "No telling where they are, ahead or behind us. We'll just stay with the traffic and hope we don't meet them again."

"They're going to be there someplace."

When they entered the traffic flow on I-90 Bob kept the speed at 70. He wondered if they had managed to lose the thugs. He glanced occasionally at Lillian, now silently gazing out of the window. He admired her bearing; her composure held even with the stress and fear. She was a special person, he thought.

Bob stared into the rear-view mirror. "Damn it…" A dark car was pacing them, about 300 yards back, too far to tell if it was the Monte Carlo.

"What? Is it them?" Lillian strained to see something out of her side mirror.

"Can't really tell. Wait until they get closer."

"God, they're going to do something. They wouldn't just follow us forever." Lillian looked again in the mirror. "What'll we do?" Her voice cracked.

"This is a well traveled highway; don't know if they want to risk much where they can be seen."

She stared into her side mirror. "They're coming closer."

Bob nodded. "Yeah, there's a break in the traffic. There coming up to look us over. Crouch down so they don't see you. They may have already seen you in the mirror."

The Monte Carlo pulled alongside. The heavily tinted windows prevented Bob from seeing inside. The car stayed next to them for a few hundred yards, and then slowly dropped behind them.

Lillian sat back up. "Oh God, what are they doing?"

"They're looking us over, trying to figure out what to do. You're right, though. They won't follow us forever."

"Bob, what are we going to do? I'm scared."

Just then they heard a clear voice on the CB radio. "Hey there buddy in maroon Dodge camper truck, you listening? Come back."

Bob picked up the microphone. "Copy, driver, go ahead."

"Y'all having a problem with the Monte Carlo? He's been on your tail for a long time. I'm about 1/8-mile behind him."

"They've been chasing us since Janesville."

"I'll be back here if you need help."

"Thanks, driver. I really appreciate it."

Bob looked over at Lillian who stared at him in surprise. She looked again into her side mirror.

"What are they going to do?" Lillian's look pleaded for an answer.

"Well, at least we have one friend back there. I'm assuming the goons don't have a CB radio"

"When we stop… Bob, I'm afraid."

"We'll look for a safe place in a while," said Bob, again checking the mirror.

Lillian nervously looked in the rear-view mirror, but the car remained behind them. She began to speak again of her life with Joey.

"Yeah, I was just there for when he wanted me. After a while he didn't even come home for supper. He didn't want to have to talk to me about anything he was doing. He even stopped bringing his friends around. He got real paranoid, accused me of talking to the FBI. He would slap me around, accusing me and trying to get me to say that I had talked to them. He threatened to kill me if he found out I had ratted him out."

"You should have left long ago," said Bob.

"I was too scared to. I knew what he had done to people that crossed him. He bragged about it when he had a few too many. It made me sick that people we had known and cared about had suddenly disappeared."

Bob shook his head, glanced at the mirror. No one was close behind.

"I was making myself ill. I couldn't find any peace, not even with my priest. He just told me to hang in there, to stay with him, that it was the right thing to do. After a while, I figured out that Joey was giving him some big contributions – bought him off."

"What did your doctor say? Did you have a regular doctor?"

"Yes, I went to the doctor a few times a year for one thing or another. He gave me some medicine to calm me, but I hated it. I just felt like a zombie. He did suggest I get out of my marriage and far away from Chicago. He said to just disappear and start a new life."

"I think the doc had the right idea." Bob glanced at her.

She met his glance. "I gave it a lot of thought, but I was always so afraid. He had threatened me and I knew that he could do it, that he could kill me. I don't think he has a soul, not and be in that business." She turned to look out of the window, her hands clutched together in her lap.

"Don't punish yourself, Lillian. You *are* out of there and we'll beat this thing. You'll see." Bob glanced at her and smiled. He reached for her hand and they held on tightly.

They were quiet for a while. Bob had finished the dregs of his coffee and wished he had more, but he didn't want to stop. He saw now that the car behind him was coming up rapidly.

"Here they come again," he said.

Lillian looked in her side mirror. "They're right behind us."

The Monte Carlo pulled up alongside the truck camper. The horn blared twice and the darkened window then lowered a few inches. Bob saw an arm jut out holding a pistol, gesturing with it for Bob to pull over. A shudder of fear temporarily paralyzed him. He focused on keeping the truck on a straight course. The horn sounded again and the passenger again waved the pistol. Bob held the truck straight in his lane and otherwise ignored them. A bead of sweat formed on his brow. Suddenly the car shot forward and swerved into Bob's lane, forcing him to swerve and touch the brakes.

"Son of a bitch!" hissed Bob.

"What are they doing?" she cried out.

The car swerved back into the inside lane, just ahead of the truck. The hand at the window again gestured rapidly with the pistol for Bob to pull over. Bob tensed, ready for another attempt to get him to stop. There was a loud bang. Lillian cried out. It took a couple seconds for Bob to realize that the gun had been fired. The car lurched forward again and swerved into their lane. Bob was ready, tapping the brakes, keeping the truck straight in his lane.

"God!" gasped Lillian, "They're going to kill us!"

The car swerved back into the inside lane and drifted back a few hundred feet behind them.

"Hey, camper buddy, still out there? Come back." The driver's voice came through loud and clear.

"I'm here. We had a little trouble with the goons in the Monte Carlo. They fired a gun, trying to get us to stop. They'll hurt us bad if we do."

"We don't want that to happen. Stand by."

"10-4, driver."

Lillian looked at Bob, fear evident on her face. "What should we do?" she asked weakly.

"We sure aren't stopping for those jerks," replied Bob. He checked the mirror again, the car was holding its distance.

"Camper buddy, come back."

"I'm here, that you behind the Monte Carlo?"

"That's a 10-4, about 300 feet behind them. We got two Hutchinson Freight rigs back here. We've been on the road just over the legal limit and we're holing up at the Big Prairie Truck Stop at Sioux Falls. Might be a good idea for you-all to park your rig there, we'll park next to you. We'll be there until dawn. Copy all that?"

"Copy. We'll do that. Thank you."

"When you get there, pull into the truck lot. I'll pull in right behind you and my buddy will be next to you. Come back."

"Copy. Thanks again."

Bob again checked the mirror; the car was still well behind him.

"I saw a sign a while ago for Big Prairie Truck Stop in Sioux Falls. It's just inside South Dakota. It must be a big place. We'll arrive 5 to 5:30."

"Stay there overnight, like the driver said?" she asked.

"I'm thinking it's a good idea. I'm not sure that those goons want to mess with a couple of truckers."

"They'll try to hit us tonight. Oh God, this is so terrible…putting you in so much danger."

"We'll be okay." He smiled at her, but his stomach didn't feel right.

The next hour was uneventful. The car stayed behind them. Bob could see one of the Hutchinson Freight rigs behind the car.

"Hey, camper buddy, Big Prairie is two miles ahead."

"Thanks, driver. We'll be pulling in there."

"10-4."

Soon Bob signaled his turn into Big Prairie Truck Stop. Coming off the exit ramp it was evident that this was a huge facility. Several fueling bays were in front of the building to service cars. Another row of bays could be seen on the opposite side where the truck parking was designated.

Bob turned into Truck and RV Parking and slowed as he looked for a favorable parking place. He saw the black Monte Carlo hesitate and then go into the automobile parking area.

"Boy, this place *is* big," commented Lillian.

"Sure is."

Bob chose a parking spot close to the building. A red Hutchinson rig pulled in behind him, filling his rear view mirror, and stopped with a hissing release of air. In less than a minute the other Hutchinson truck pulled into the parking space next to him.

"We got ya covered, camper buddy," came over the CB radio.

"We really appreciate it."

Bob and Lillian got out of the truck as the drivers from the two Hutchinson rigs came toward them. They were big burly men, somewhat overweight, but exuding an air of no-nonsense.

"Hi folks. I'm Tim Olsen, the guy chatting with you. This is George Schneider. He was behind me. We're out of Pittsburgh." They both grinned and extended their hands.

Bob shook hands with them. "This is Lillian and I'm Bob. We really appreciate your help. We're dealing with a couple of crazy goons I think would just as soon kill us."

Tim looked at Bob with some skepticism. "Well, we didn't know what to make of it. It looked pretty dangerous. The Monte Carlo pulled into the parking area. Can't see it from here, though."

"What's the problem, if you don't mind us asking?" George looked at them curiously.

"It's a convoluted story," Bob started, "but the short version is that back in Illinois there was an altercation where Lillian was threatened and assaulted by her boss in a diner. I happened to be in there at the time and basically knocked the dirt bag out for a while. She escaped by hiding in my camper. The problem is this guy is a cousin of her ex, and they are both in the mob. I think the guys in the car were sent out to kill Lillian. Me too, probably. They figure she knows too much about them. They won't tolerate her running off."

George looked at Tim, a knowing glance between them. "Where you from Bob?'

"I used to live in Lowell, Mass. I'm driving out to visit my cousin in Montana. I'm retired."

Tim nodded. "That's something I'd like to do soon, get me an RV and be gone for a while."

George spoke up again. "You know, we heard on the CB back a ways something about trouble at a diner in Rockford." George smiled. "Don't suppose you folks know about that, huh?" [you said earlier Bob didn't hear anything about it on the CB. Therefore, George couldn't have heard about it either without Bob overhearing the conversation. They might know about the diner from other conversations in the past and know it to be an unsavory place.] Not so. The CB only reaches a few miles, typically. So what one heard isn't likely to be what the other heard or didn't hear.

Bob replied. "Yeah, that was us."

"We don't stop there. We know the guys there are mob. They must be paying off the sheriff." He turned to Lillian. "You worked there?"

Lillian nodded. "I needed a job. He turned out to be a real bastard."

George responded. "Yeah, we heard that from some other guys."

Lillian looked at Bob. Bob scratched his head. "We don't know what we'll do after Montana. It depends on what happens with the guys following us. I can't believe they let us come this far. They're a long way from home. I think they're crazy enough to try to wreck us or hit us when we're stopped - put a couple of slugs in us."

Tears formed in Lillian's eyes and she blinked trying to hold them back. Tim looked at her and said, "Look, let's get you by tonight. Tomorrow is another day. You'll be okay parked here."

"Thanks. Sure appreciate your help," said Bob. "Want us to bring you anything?"

"No…Why don't you two go inside and get some supper. We'll hang out here until you get back," suggested Tim. "We'll eat later."

"Okay." Bob looked at Lillian, she nodded. "We'll go now, meet you back here."

"Take your time. We'll keep an eye out for the two clowns in the Monte Carlo," replied George.

Lillian and Bob hurried towards the entrance and found a mob in front of the concessions. Bob looked for the restroom signs and spotted them in the hallway connecting to a restaurant. He quickly scanned the crowd but didn't see anyone suspicious. Lillian looked nervously at Bob.

He tried to reassure her. "A big crowd is good. If they're in here, I don't know where. They could be in the other section where the showers and telephones are. I think there are stores too, in the back - big place."

"Do you want to eat in here or sit down somewhere?" asked Lillian.

"Yeah, look…over at the end. That's a sit-down place. See it? Elmer's CharBroil."

"Okay, let's go there. I'm buying, remember?" She smiled at him.

After a brief stop at the restrooms, they went into the restaurant.

The young hostess sat them immediately and handed them the menu. "Marge will be right with you" she said pleasantly.

Lillian looked at Bob. "What are you having?"

Bob noticed an older heavy woman approached them. She pulled out the order pad from her apron, smoothing it back down around her girth. He glanced at her face, wrinkled with a time worn expression. She had been at this job too long, Bob thought.

She forced a smile, "Hi, I'm Marge. Something to drink?"

"Do you have a Sam Adams?" he asked. [I thought Sam was local. This is a long way from their bailiwick, isn't it?] Using some license here.

"Yes, we do. Just started carrying it."

Lillian looked at Bob. "You know, I've never had one of those. I'll try one."

A minute later Marge brought the two beers.

Lillian tasted hers and smiled. "Pretty good."

"I kinda like it," Bob replied, "calories and all."

"Are you ready to order?" asked Marge.

"Lillian?"

"Oh, the roast beef dinner for me and a salad with ranch dressing."

The waitress turned her attention to Bob. "I'd like the BBQ beef sandwich and a salad, vinegar and oil," he said.

Marge smiled, picked up the menus and headed toward the swinging doors of the kitchen.

"This should be better than one of the burger joints," commented Bob.

Lillian nodded in agreement. "I'm glad we did this. It was nice of those drivers to wait for us to have supper. They didn't have to do that."

"There are still some nice people in the world," added Bob.

The waitress arrived with their salads and bread.

Lillian slowly put her fork down on her plate and looked up at Bob. Her lips trembled.

"Bob, I should take a bus tomorrow and disappear, maybe then they will leave you alone." She looked at him with sadness.

"Where would you go? You don't know who would be willing to hide you. You can't go to relatives where they'd find you anyway." Bob spoke softly, hoping she would listen to reasoning.

"But I have no right to do this to you." Tears welled in her eyes. She looked away.

"I have no place special to be. I'm going to stop at my cousin's place for a while. I don't know how long, or even where I'll go after that. But I'd like it very much if you would go with me, no strings attached. We don't *have* to let these jerks win. I think in time we'll figure something out. In the meantime we just have to be careful."

Marge arrived with their meals.

"Smells good," said Lillian as she reached for the salt and pepper shakers. She paused and looked at him. "Bob, I appreciate everything you're doing for me, just a stranger you found in your camper."

Bob smiled. "You're certainly not a stranger any more."

She looked at him, her eyes searching his face. "I like being with you. You're a good man."

"Let's keep heading west, see how this plays out with those goons, okay?"

"Okay," she nodded.

Bob looked quickly around the parking lot as they left the restaurant. He didn't see the Monte Carlo parked well back in the lot. He also didn't see the two men who were leaning against a pickup truck, and who started toward them as soon as they came into the trucker's parking area. Angelo and Lou caught up to Bob and Lillian when they were about fifty feet from the camper. Lou, the younger one, grabbed Bob tightly by the arm.

"Come on, pop. Let's take a walk."

When Angelo took Lillian's arm, she screamed. Bob swiveled on his feet, driving his free fist into the younger man's stomach with as much force as he could muster. He heard Lou gasp for air, and his grip loosened. Bob broke free and swung around, landing his fist hard against the hoodlum's face. Bob heard Lillian scream again.

"All right, hold it!" The two burly truck drivers were approaching, both with wooden clubs. They smacked the truncheons into their palms as they approached. "Take your hands off her!" Tim bellowed.

Angelo, startled, turned toward the truckers. Lillian broke loose from his grip and started toward the drivers. When Angelo moved to grab Lillian again, Tim swung his club, landing it with a thud against the side of Angelo's head. He reeled backwards, stumbled, and got back on his feet. Tim was on him quickly. "Back off asshole – your hands where I can see them."

Lou let go of Bob, reached under his jacket and pulled out a gun. But before he brought it to bear, George landed his club hard against Lou's arm. The pistol fell to the pavement. Lou roared in rage and pain, and turned toward George. The next blow landed on the side of his head, and Lou went down to his knees. Angelo went to Lou's side, pocketed the pistol, and helped him up.

"You assholes want more? We got more," said George slapping the club into his palm as he and Tim took a step closer to the two thugs.

Angelo and Lou backed away. Angelo yelled back, "You're dead! Both of you - dead!" He waved his finger at Lillian and Bob. Angelo turned and helped Lou move through the parked vehicles, disappearing into the back of the parking lot.

Bob went to Lillian. She was sobbing, her face distorted in fear. "We're okay," he said as she composed herself.

Bob turned to the two truck drivers, standing in front of the camper. "God, we really owe you guys. Thank so much."

"Hey buddy, no problem," Tim smiled broadly.

"Thank you," said Lillian, wiping her tears.

"You're sure welcome ma'am," said George. "We'll go and eat. Gotta call in, get a shower, stuff like that. I think you two should go back inside, have some coffee or dessert and wait for us to get done. We'll be in the truckers' lounge out back, but we'll come get you when we're done. It'll take us an hour or so." George looked at Tim, who nodded.

"Sure. Okay. It's a good idea," said Bob. He stepped away from Lillian, suddenly embarrassed to have been holding her. She held onto his arm.

Tim and George went down the hall under the red neon *Truckers' Lounge* sign, while Lillian and Bob took a seat where they could see everyone coming into the food court. Bob then walked to the McDonalds counter and brought back coffee and two large bags of French fries.

She looked at him, "What are we going to do? They won't give up."

"No…not before they get what they came for. We're parked in a good place, but I'll keep watch. If I doze off, wake me if you hear anything.

"But tomorrow…?"

He wasn't sure what to say, and wasn't sure what would really happen in the morning.

"Lillian, we'll work through this."

She reached across the table, placed her hand over his, and looked into his face. "I'm afraid of what they can do," she said. "I shouldn't have taken that stuff. That was so insane."

"You wanted to escape. You needed money. You didn't know what else was in the bag."

"God, I had to take *that* bag."

"I wish we could just give it back to them." for the twentieth time. It's getting boring."

"They threatened me so many times. I'm sure they meant it. Yes, they want the bag, but I don't think they're going to let me live, if I know Joey and Vinny."

"Maybe if we hold on to the bag, we can use it as a bargaining chip later. Anyhow, there are two of us now, and the truckers. It's not as easy as they might have thought."

She squeezed his hand. "I think I might like you." A small grin lit up her face.

———

Angelo slammed the car door shut and turned toward Lou. "What the hell you thinking, pulling a gun in front of those truckers?"

"I want to finish this, goddamn it!"

"We can't just kill them. Not yet. Not before I get my hands on Vinny's CD and book," exclaimed Angelo, rubbing his sore head. "Christ, this hurts."

"Damn near broke my arm, can hardly move it! I should go kill those bastards." Lou moved to open the car door.

Angelo didn't like the crazed look in Lou's eyes. "Stay here, damn it!" He rubbed the side of his head.

The cell phone in Angelo's pocket started ringing. He reached for it and flipped it open.

"Yeah?" Angelo knew who would be calling.

"You got my stuff, yet?" Vinny's voice sent a chill down his back.

"We just got to them at this truck stop, but a couple of truckers came to their aid when the bitch screamed. It coulda got bad, lots of people around. But, we're back in the car comin' up with another plan."

"What are you saying?" Vinny roared into the phone. "That you had them and let them go?"

Angelo tried to reason. "We were going to take them to the car…do it there…outa sight…then look for your stuff in their camper. A couple truckers started beating on us with tire clubs. They really hurt Lou. He can hardly use his arm. We had to let go of her and the old fart. We couldn't just off them in the parking lot."

"Listen and listen well. I want that disk and my book. You finish the job tomorrow. I don't care where it is, parking lot or in church…you get it done. I don't pay you two candy-asses to tour the country. Get it done! You hearin' me?"

"Yeah, Vinny, I hear you. We'll finish the job tomorrow." Angelo's stomach was in knots. He closed the cell phone and turned to Lou.

"If we don't finish this tomorrow, we'll be next on his list."

"All right, we'll do it my way tomorrow," said Lou, patting the pistol under his jacket.

"Angelo scowled. "We'll do it the *right* way. I ain't goin' back to prison."

—

Bob poured two cups of coffee and then sat at the table. Lillian nervously looked out of the camper window, her view totally blocked by a Hutchinson Freight truck.

"We're so lucky that these two guys came along to help us," said Lillian.

"Yes indeed. Those jerks don't want to mess with these guys. They've seen a lot in their life, I'm sure, and the likes of those two punks probably isn't a big challenge for them."

"I'm glad we're here next to them."

"Lillian, if we get to bed early we could be ready to leave here when the truckers leave. I imagine that they'll be out of here before dawn. Want to do that? I could ask them about it."

Lillian's eyes seemed to light up. "Sure."

"Okay, I'll go talk to them."

Bob left the camper and spotted George leaning on his cab with a cigarette.

"How you two doin? Catching my last smoke. Don't like smokin' in the cab."

"We were wondering if we could leave here in the morning when you do and go down the road in front of you?"

George scratched his head. "Don't see why not. We run at 75, you got to do at least that."

Bob nodded. "Okay, I can do that. Really appreciate it."

"All right, I'll tell Tim. See you at 6 sharp. We can't wait for you, it's got to be 6."

"Okay, 6 it is."

CHAPTER 7 PURSUIT

They lay dozing in the dark, awakening with a start when a flash of headlights lit up the camper, or from a loud release of air brakes nearby. Bob got up and went to the windows a few times, parting the curtains, and then lay back down. Their eyes glistened in the sweep of the occasional headlights, before the darkness again enveloped them and they dozed. Someone coughed and Lillian bolted upright banging her head on the ceiling.

"Bob…Bob…did you hear that?" she whispered.

"Shhh." Bob went to each window, staring into the darkness. Only the dim light from running lights of dozens of trucks gave any illumination.

"A couple of drivers smoking out there, not the two goons." Bob turned back to his bed.

"What time is it?"

"Just after 1. A few more hours to go."

"Get any sleep?" she asked.

"Not much."

"Me neither."

Bob just got to sleep when the alarm went off at 5 a.m. He dressed quickly and called to Lillian, awakening her. They went together into the building and hurried through their bathroom routines. Bob waited outside the women's restroom for her, and then hurried to the food concession area. Bob looked at his watch.

"It's 5:30 already, we better hurry. What can I get you for breakfast? We'll just take it with us." Bob looked at Lillian as she stared at the menu posters. *She is lovely*, he thought. His eyes surreptitiously dropped over her figure, today clad in a patterned blouse and jeans that fit like a glove.

"Oh, I think an EggMcMuffin and coffee will do me." She glanced at him while he quickly averted his gaze.

Bob nodded, "Okay, sounds good. Stay close, in case they come in." Bob moved to the McDonalds counter and placed his order. Lillian looked around nervously, but there were few people in the food court at the early hour. It took only a couple of minutes and Bob had a bag of food and a tray with two large coffees.

"Wow! What'd you get?" asked Lillian as she eyed the two bags.

"I got two EggMcMuffins and two bear claw pastries." He smiled as he handed her the bags and held onto the coffees.

"Well, there goes my diet," she said smiling.

"Mine too, unless they left the cholesterol out of it."

At the condiment counter he stuffed coffee creamer packets and napkins into his jacket pocket. Outside of the building everything looked quiet in the early light. They hurried toward the camper and were ready to leave at 5:47. Bob started the truck, and after a few seconds turned on the headlights and started to leave the parking place. Tim and George had their engines purring with the running lights on. Tim flashed his headlights as Bob and Lillian pulled away. Bob waved and then moved toward the parking lot exit.

He saw no other vehicles moving in the parking lot and couldn't see the Monte Carlo. He felt sure they were there, and also sure that the two goons would be behind them shortly. He sensed that today the risk would increase, that the thugs would be angry and desperate. How could he put an end to these crazy events? He felt bad for Lillian, to have to live with this threat. It seemed so extraordinary to send two goons cross-country to stop her. Stop her from what? Of course, he didn't really know just what kind of threat the information in the book and on the CD posed to the Vinny and Joey characters. He'd have to play it a day at a time, hope for the best. Accelerating onto I-90, he set his speed at 75.

Lillian handed Bob an EggMcMuffin and poured his coffee into his insulated cup and secured the lid.

"Thanks. I *am* a little hungry."

"Me too. I might eat that bear claw after all." She smiled at him.

She'd been fighting with herself since she woke up, thinking the right thing to do would be to get on a bus and disappear. But to where? Did she dare trust any of her few friends? Would she have to go into the witness protection program with the FBI? Then what? She had mulled it over all night, staring into the darkness. Guilt plagued her when she thought of the danger she was bringing to Bob. She glanced at him now with fondness. *They don't make too many like him*, she thought. His appreciative glances had made her feel good. He was a trim and attractive man and he could easily pass as ten years younger. It would be difficult to leave him now when, every day, she felt closer to him. But she couldn't keep him in danger. How could she live with herself if he was injured or killed?

The sun was up behind them. It appeared to be a nice day, without a cloud in the sky. Bob did not see anything alarming when he glanced at the rear view mirrors. The only traffic so far had been trucks that zoomed passed him well over the speed limit. He saw another truck on the rear horizon now, and he reached up to adjust the volume on the CB radio.

"You ready for your dessert?" asked Lillian. She handed him a Bear Claw in a napkin. "It's a little sticky."

"Thanks. I'm surprised, the Big M coffee isn't bad," he commented.

"Yeah, I was surprised too. Used to be you could hardly drink it."

"Good morning camper buddy. Got your ears on?" The CB radio grabbed their attention. Bob pulled the microphone from the ceiling hook.

"Copy. Still munching on breakfast. Is 75 okay?"

"Inch it up some. Keep it between 75 and 80. We're behind you about half a mile. Haven't seen the bandits yet."

"Hoping I can finish my coffee before they show up."

"Okay, leave you to it. Breaker you when they come past me."

"10-4."

Lillian looked over at Bob. "It's so good to know they're back there."

Bob nudged the truck up to 78. "Yes indeed, swell guys."

Lillian looked down at her lap. She spoke calmly. "Bob, they're going to keep coming after me. I know it. It isn't right for me to do this to you. It's not your fight. I think it would be best if you dropped me at a bus station when they're not around. Then I could disappear. They wouldn't know where. I'd figure something out." She didn't look at him.

He couldn't argue with her logic. But what he felt was something else, an attraction and a sense of caring that seemed both strange and welcome. He cared and knew there was no point in denying it, at least not to himself.

"I think if we stick together, we have a good chance of beating this. Those two truckers are going clear to Tacoma; we could stick with them." Bob's calm voice didn't betray the panic he felt. He didn't want her to disappear from his life.

"You shouldn't have to be in danger because of me. It's not fair to you." She still didn't look up. He glanced at her, but just then the CB radio came alive.

"Wake up camper buddy! Bandits headed your way. They just passed me. We'll be closing the distance to you."

"Thanks, driver. Let's see what they're up to." A glance out of his side mirror showed the Monte Carlo about to overtake him on the inside. The passenger side window was rolled down.

"What are those bastards going to do?" She strained to look out of the driver's window.

The car pulled up next to them and the man on the passenger side gestured forcibly with the gun in his hand for Bob to pull off the road. Bob ignored him and kept the truck in his lane. The car spurted forward and swerved in front of the camper. Bob touched the brake but held the truck steady. The car swerved back to the inside lane and dropped back even with the camper. The horn blared from the car. Bob saw the passenger point the pistol at him. Bob touched the brake and heard the loud bang. He swerved the truck to get behind the car. Another shot came from the car ahead, but passed by harmlessly. The car swerved into the outside lane and Bob touched the brake, swerving to stay behind him.

"Get your head down!"

Lillian dropped flat on the seat.

Bob picked up the CB microphone. "Breaker drivers! We got a situation here. Bandit is trying to force us off the road. He's fired two shots! Come back."

Bob pressed his hand against Lillian's shoulder, keeping her down against the seat.

"Copy, camper buddy. As soon as traffic clears *behind* us, we're gonna do a cleanup operation. Let these two cars go by, and then I'm coming up next to you and will pull in front of those clowns. The second driver will pass you, and as soon as he does, you put on the brakes and give him room. It'll be over in a few seconds. You copy?"

"Copy that."

"Okay. Stay alert. Here goes."

"What…what's happening?" Lillian was wide eyed, mouth agape. She pushed herself upright, grabbed the hand-grips and stared at the truck as it roared past them. There was an intimidating blast of the horn as the truck overtook the Monte Carlo.

Bob and Lillian saw the second truck come up beside them. Bob glanced at the rear-view mirror. There was no traffic in view. He braced himself. As soon as the trailer passed, he applied the brakes. A dozen car lengths opened between him and the Monte Carlo. Suddenly, the trailer of the second truck swerved to the right forcing the Monte Carlo onto the shoulder. When they tried to get back onto the pavement, the wheels of the trailer slammed against the car. There was a screeching howl and a cloud of dust as the truck driver forced his rig farther into the lane. The car went off the road, did a 180-degree turn as it dug into the gravel, rolled over twice and landed on its side against the wire fence. Bob and Lillian could no longer see the car. It disappeared behind them. Lillian craned her neck to see it in her mirror, but an explosion of dust engulfed the overturned car.

"Breaker, camper buddy. Operation completed."

"Wow! We owe you a lot - very grateful."

"You're welcome. They won't bother you any more. We'll call it in to smoky as a one-car crash."

"Thank you, both."

"We're going to put the hammer down and roll. You two are okay. Enjoy life."

"Thank you." Bob hung up the microphone.

"I can't believe what just happened," said Lillian in wide-eyed astonishment. "Those guys are gone?"

Bob smiled. "They sure are. Pretty beat up, I imagine. We won't see those two again."

"I can hardly believe it. Suddenly they're gone?" She twisted her body to look in the rear view mirror, but saw nothing. "Vinny will know that something happened. He and Joey will do *something*. They have the money to buy anyone." Lillian stared into the mirror again.

"Lillian." Bob spoke softly.

She turned toward him.

"They're gone." He spoke softly. "There may be others later, but it won't be for a day or so. We're okay for now." He glanced at her, saw tears in her eyes.

She turned in her seat and reached over to him, kissed his cheek. "Thank you." Lillian sat quietly and stared at the countryside, occasionally wiping her eyes with the back of her hand.

—

Dust swirled in through the open window. Lou sputtered and reached to his face, felt the sticky blood. He wiped his hand across his eyes. His vision, blurred with blood and dirt, cleared for a moment then clouded over again. He moved his hand to the gash on his forehead, wet and painful. He felt Angelo under him. Without their seat belts, they had careened about the interior of the car as it had spun and rolled after the impact with the truck. Lou now lay on top of Angelo, whose bloody face pressed against the closed driver's window.

"Angelo!" The sound croaked from Lou's throat. He moved his jaw open and closed, gasping with the pain. It hurt to breath. He took shallow breaths. His moved his hand over his chest and when he touched the lower ribs, he cried out in pain.

"Shit…shit…shit." He again wiped the dust and blood from his eyes. Pops and creaking noises came from under the car. The smell of gasoline wafted to his nostrils. He didn't hear the motor running, but fearfully he reached to the ignition key on the steering column and turned it off.

Angelo moaned, grabbed the steering wheel with his right hand, and tried to pull himself to a different position. He cried out and slumped back to where he had been.

"Angelo! Christ! You alive?" Lou mumbled the words through closed jaw.

"Get the hell off me…get off me," Angelo gasped.

"I'll try to open my door. Oh shit, it hurts. My ribs." Lou mumbled, as he worked to brace his leg against the center shifter console. He pushed his leg muscles, slowly at first, then harder until his hands reached the window sill of his door. Slowly, and with considerable agony, he straightened his legs, and pulled himself erect, his head now out the window.

He heard several cars drive by at a high rate of speed, but could not focus his eyes to see them.

"Don't stop, assholes," he muttered. Who would help them, he wondered.

Lou turned his head toward the highway when he heard the loud bark of a Jake brake. He wiped at his eyes and made out the blurry outline of a big rig pulling to a stop on the shoulder. He clung to the door, unable to get much breath. He heard Angelo moan, then try to say something.

"Angelo, someone's stopping."

Truck doors slammed shut, and in a few seconds two men were peering into the car. One moved to look closely at Lou.

"Holy shit! Charlie, call it in! This guy ain't lookin' good."

Charlie stooped to look through the shattered windshield, then backed up and pulled his cell phone from his hip. He was able to reach a 911 operator.

"Pete, someone called it in a couple minutes ago. Anyhow, smoky should be here in a few minutes. Told 'em to send an ambulance."

"Hey, guy, help is coming. What's your name? Mine's Charlie."

Lou tried to focus on who was talking. The man was a blur. He blinked his eyes a few times, and could then make out his face.

"I'm Lou. Truck hit us, cut us off."

"Okay. Don't talk. Cop'll be here in a couple minutes. Your friend doesn't look real good, he's conscious though. Don't want to move you, let the pros do that."

"Pete, the driver looks pretty beat up. He's barely conscious." Charlie peered again through the shattered windshield Pete shook his head. "Damn! This car really took a beating. Goddamn hotdog driver is probably to hell and gone by now."

"Yeah, maybe someone got a plate number," mumbled Charlie. "Hey, here comes smoky."

A Highway Patrol car stopped behind the trailer truck, emergency lights flashing. The officer hurried down to the wreck, quickly assessed the condition of the two trapped men, spoke a few words with the truck drivers, and then hurried back to his patrol car.

"Cop's gonna call for help," said Charlie to no one in particular.

The state patrolman returned shortly and took notes on what information the drivers could offer. A fire-rescue van and an EMT vehicle arrived six minutes later from a local town. A quick assessment was made, and the EMT supervisor alerted Sioux Falls on the condition of the two men. A decision was made to use Medivac to Sioux Falls, because the nearby farming towns were not well enough equipped to handle serious injuries and the battery of tests that would have to be performed. Fire-Rescue removed the windshield and the passenger door, and ten minutes later the EMT team had removed the two men from the car. Charlie and Pete bade farewell to the policeman and were on their way.

Lou and Angelo were attended to in the ambulance while waiting for the helicopter. Meantime, the state patrolman, David Cooper, inspected and documented the crash site and details of the vehicle. A loaded 9-mm and a 22-caliber automatic pistol were recovered from the car and bagged. The registration and insurance papers were also bagged. An inspection of the driver's license of both men was made, and inquiry sent to NCIC. The patrolman watched as the wrecker people began to load the car onto a flatbed truck, but glanced at his computer screen frequently.

"There's more to these guys, I'm sure," he mumbled.

Cooper didn't have to wait long. A report on Angelo Fontana appeared first. He had been released from Joliet 18 months ago having served a five year stint for armed robbery. There were no outstanding warrants. Place of employment was listed as Lawndale Truck Stop. Supervisor was listed as Vincent DiCosta.

A minute later a report on Lou DiMatto appeared on the screen. Several arrests for disorderly conduct, and a felony arrest for assault and battery for which he did a year in county lockup. There were no outstanding warrants. No employment information was available.

"Where have I heard the DiCosta name before?" he asked himself. Then he typed another inquiry. The reply stated Vincent DiCosta reported through Michael Santos into the Frank Cappella outfit in Chicago.

"Yeah," said Copper aloud, "I remember that name. Nasty prick."

Cooper typed out a message to his sergeant as the Medivac helicopter landed nearby.

CHAPTER 8 DECISION AT BUTTE

Bob pushed on for over an hour at 80 mph with some satisfaction, putting distance between them and the car wreck. Were they dead? He didn't care. There had been a few mentions of a single-car wreck on westbound I-90 on the CB, but otherwise it had turned into a quiet morning. He looked at Lillian, who was gazing at the rolling hills and new grass of spring. She seemed to be at peace for the moment; the stress lines all too common on her face were absent. He felt a need to hold her, but dismissed it and turned back to look at the highway.

She began talking again about the troubled life she had while married to Joey.

Bob asked, "Why didn't you leave him? I mean, long before divorcing him?"

"I was afraid. I believed the threats he made. All our friends were really *his* friends, and I couldn't expect any help."

"Why'd you take that bag with the CD and book from Vinny's safe? Why not just walk out of there? It would've gone easier on you."

She nodded. "It would have been the smart thing to do. I didn't have any money with me and I knew he kept some in the safe. It was just my luck to pick up the one bag where he hid his secret stuff. I'm sorry."

"You don't have anything to apologize for, not to me."

Before crossing the Missouri River, Bob exited I-90 and drove into the town of Chamberlain. He spotted the Burger King sign and pulled into the parking lot. He looked over at Lillian. "I need some more coffee. Can I get you anything?"

She turned to him. "I'm coming in with you, at least to use the rest room."

"Sure." Bob got out of the truck and went to her door and opened it.

She stepped out onto the pavement. As he reached around her to close the door, she pressed against him. Her arms went around his neck; his encircled her waist. She hugged him and then her mouth found his. She kissed him tenderly and then laid her head against his shoulder, hugging him even closer.

"Thank you. Thank you for being there for me."

"I'm glad I was; glad that I know you," he replied, his heart pounding.

"Me too." She broke away and took his arm, tugging him toward the Burger King.

Looking forward to a break after driving all day at speeds sometimes over 80 mph, Bob turned off the highway at the Badlands National Park. He stopped in front of the headquarters building and museum. It was early evening but the sky was still bright in the lengthening daylight hours. The view was expansive; the lonesome high plains, he thought. They had seen many grazing antelope during the day, and many more sadly crushed on the highway by the big rigs during the previous night. Lillian had been upset by the sight of the antelope carcasses, had pointed excitedly at all the grazing antelope she saw. Here, on the bluff of the Badlands Headquarters, a steady wind blew. Bob looked up and, pointed at an eagle riding the air currents.

Lillian shaded her eyes. "It is so raw here, yet beautiful. So quiet. Only the wind," remarked Lillian.

"This is the high plains, a tough place in winter." He saw the faraway look, the half-smile as she gazed into the distance. His heart went out to her, knowing the deep seated fear that was her constant company.

"I'd love to spend a little time looking through the museum. Want to?" she asked.

He hesitated before replying. "Probably closed at this hour. Let's get through the Black Hills and then stop for the night. We've come a really long way today."

"Okay. I'll just grab a couple sodas out of the machine."

Sundance, Wyoming, a small town on the high plains, lay against the hills overlooking I-90 and the broad valley west of the Black Hills and the Badlands. Bob saw the sign for Hillside Campground and took the exit. There was a red glow on the western horizon as they pulled into the campground. High on a hill, it offered a good vantage point without being readily seen from the highway. He didn't expect any trouble, though, not for a few days at least.

Lillian looked off into the darkening landscape. "Beautiful," she commented.

"You have to be pretty hardy to live out here. Except for these small towns, there are just ranches and a few oil wells."

"Yeah, but I kinda like it," she added.

Bob walked up to her. "Like to find a *real* restaurant tonight? I can ask at the office, see what they suggest."

"That would be neat, I'm buying, though." She gave him a good-natured, stern look.

He smiled. "I'll be right back." He walked off toward the office building.

Bob was back in a few minutes. "This little town has several restaurants. They're along the main street. There are a couple of dives but their favorite place is the Sundance Bar and Grill. Apparently it's an old place that's been in the same family for ages. The folks in the office say it's unpretentious but has the best food around."

"I'm convinced. Let's give it a try." Lillian smiled broadly. "Give me a couple of minutes and I'll be ready."

Bob stood looking at the broad vista while Lillian remained in the camper. *Maybe I'm a little crazy, but I really do like her. I would sure hate to see here go.* He thought of her elegant bearing, her throaty voice and her appealing personality. Letting go would be difficult.

He turned when he heard the camper door open. Lillian stepped out. She had brushed out her shoulder length hair, and had changed into dark slacks with a tight fitting long-sleeve white blouse. *She is beautiful,* he thought.

"You look very nice." He felt his face getting warm.

"Thank you," she smiled.

"I should maybe get out of these jeans," he said.

"No, don't. I like the way you look. Come on, let's find that place." She took his arm and they went to the door of the truck. He opened it and helped her in.

They left the campground and descended the hillside to the main street. About a mile to the west, they arrived at a log cabin structure that was the Sundance Bar and Grill. The gravel lot in front was packed with cars and pick-up trucks. The hostess met them at the door. A large U-shaped bar took up nearly half the room, opening at the far wall by the kitchen. Booths lined the walls, and the hostess sat them in a corner booth. The bar stools were occupied by working men of all ages, some with sweat-stained cowboy hats, all with boots that had seen better days. Cigarettes dangled from unshaven faces. A blue haze hung over the bar. Several men turned to admire Lillian for a few bold seconds. There were a number of middle-aged patrons seated in booths and at the tables. The smell of barbecue wafted from the kitchen.

"I already like this place," said Lillian. "It feels right."

Bob smiled, "You have some admirers up at the bar."

She grinned and her eyes drifted across the room. "Look at the old stuff on the logs; pictures, and the bison head. How neat."

The hostess appeared and handed them menus. "Hello folks. Thanks for stopping in. I'd be happy to get you a drink while you check out the menu."

Bob looked up at her. "Sure, that'd be great. By the way, the folks at the campground suggested we come here."

"They're nice people. They come here often."

Lillian looked up from the menu. "I'd really like a glass of wine. Merlot."

Bob nodded, "That'll work for me, too." The hostess thanked them and moved away.

Lillian opened her menu and looked at Bob. "I'm buying, remember?"

"Okay, thanks," replied Bob.

Lillian reached across the table to place a hand over his. She looked deep into his eyes. "Thank *you*. You're very special."

Bob felt the warmth rise up from his collar. "I kinda like you, too."

A smile spread across her face. She dropped her eyes back to the menu as she let go of his hand.

"I think I'll go for a T-bone, haven't had one in a long time," said Bob.

"They have a small filet. I'd like that and a salad." She closed her menu as the waitress came to the table. She brought their wineglasses and a small carafe, and walked away with their order. Lillian raised her glass to Bob. He touched his glass to hers.

"Bob," she said softly, what will happen when we get to your cousin at the ranch? We can't stay there – can we?"

"I don't know how long to stay. I guess I'll have to get a feel for how welcome we are. It's not my cousin's ranch; they just live and work there. I guess we'll play it by ear."

She looked at him, sadness in her eyes. "I don't want to get them in any trouble, it isn't right."

"I know people in Washington and Oregon, people we can stay with. I had planned on visiting them at some point." Bob didn't sound too certain. He saw Lillian shift her eyes away. A few seconds later she turned to him.

"I have to find a place where I can disappear, where I can think this out. Maybe the FBI is my only way out of this."

He reached for her hand, held it. "We've got a few days grace from them; it'll take 'em that long to regroup. We can be at the ranch by then and figure it out there. Maybe get some new ideas from my friends."

"Maybe…"

It was a cool bright morning when they pulled out of the campground. On the main street through Sundance, they stopped at a Conoco station that also had a mini-mart. Lillian grabbed a window squeegee and cleaned off the bugs while Bob pumped gas. He stole a few surreptitious glances at her when he thought she was unaware, admiring her. He turned back to the pump to retrieve the printed receipt. *God, she is gorgeous. Fat chance though, too old for her. But, I really do like her.* As he came around the truck to go into the mini-mart, she took his arm but didn't say anything.

Inside, he filled his coffee mug, along with a Styrofoam cup for Lillian, and picked up two Bear Claw pastries. At the counter, he scanned the newspaper headlines, but decided the news from the radio would do. Near the door, he spotted a rack with maps and pulled out one for Montana. He laid five dollars on the counter and joined Lillian outside in the warm sun.

"Got a map?" asked Lillian.

"Yep, Montana. The atlas in the truck doesn't give me enough detail to find the ranch where my cousin lives."

Bob saw that Lillian had a worried look and stared away from him. "Bob, they're going to be looking for me again. I just know it. I've seen how they work."

He took her hand. She turned toward him and looked into his eyes. "I'm sorry, I…" She came against him, her head against his shoulder.

"Lillian, they don't know where we are now. We'll deal with it when we have to."

She kissed him lightly on the lips. "I'm getting to like you," she said as she headed toward the truck.

Bob turned on the radio for the news broadcast. The local station briefly went through a few of the international items and some national issues. He paid attention during the local news coverage.

"...A one-car accident yesterday on I-90, west of Sioux Falls, resulted in serious injury to both occupants. The vehicle, which had rolled several times, was a total loss. The occupants were not wearing seat belts and were flown by Medevac to a Sioux Falls hospital. The sheriff stated that the driver claimed they were forced off the road by a trailer truck..."

Bob looked over at Lillian and smiled. "Those are our two goons."

She smiled thinly. "Scary..."

"I know. We *do* need to be careful." He didn't know how he could put an end to her terror; he only knew that he would do whatever he could.

He turned up the CB radio, but there was only idle trucker chatter, and no mention of the car wreck. Bob glanced often into the rear view mirror, but there didn't seem to be any pursuit. He thought that trouble, if it came, would lie ahead of them, possibly flown in from Chicago or elsewhere. Tonight he would have to be vigilant.

—

Vinny grabbed the phone on his desk on the second ring. *About time those bastards called*, he thought.

"Vincent DeCosta?"

What the hell is this? His heart skipped a beat. He didn't recognize the business-like voice.

"Yeah. What can I do for ya?"

"I'm Dr. David Reagan, supervisor at Sioux Fall General Hospital. We have two patients here, Louis DiMatto and Angelo Fontana, victims of a highway accident. Mister Fontana asked that I call and inform you of their situation. Both men are receiving treatment for their injuries at this time."

Vinny was stunned. He didn't utter a word, his mind racing.

"Mister DiCosta, are you still there?"

"Yeah…I'm here. Sorry. It's just a shock to hear this. What happened to 'em? When'll they be released?"

"I can't give you any details. You'll want to contact the South Dakota State Police, here in Sioux Falls."

"State Police?"

"Yes. I have the contact information. Can you write it down?"

"Yeah, sure. Go ahead."

The doctor gave Vinny the name and phone number and disconnected. Vinny hung up the phone and reached in his desk drawer for the bottle of bourbon. He poured a couple fingers of the amber fluid into a stained shot glass, tipped it to his lips, and drained half of it.

"State Police?" He shook his head. "What the hell?"

Why couldn't the doctor tell him when they'd be getting outa there, he wondered. Had they been arrested?

"Gotta tell Joey." He reached for the glass. "No, better call and find out what the hell is going on."

Vinny drained the glass and reached for the bottle, splashing more into the glass and a fair amount on the desk top.

He punched in the telephone number given to him by the doctor. It was answered on the second ring.

"South Dakota State Police, Sioux Falls. Captain Eric Kohler speaking."

"Uh, yes…I was told to call you about two fellows that work for me. They were in some sort of accident. Doctor wouldn't give me any information."

"Yes, sir, and you are?"

"Uh, Vince DiCosta."

"And the two gentlemen are Louis DeMitteo and Angelo Fontana?"

"Yes…they, uh…they work for me." Vince felt a knot in his stomach. He reached for the shot glass.

"They were on a business trip?"

"No. Visiting some friends out that way. Forget where exactly."

"So you don't know where they were going?"

"I, uh, gave 'em time off. What happened to 'em?"

"The report indicates a one-car rollover accident. We're still investigating."

"The car? Is it totaled?"

"Yes, sir. It's in our impound lot at this time. It can be claimed next week if you wish, otherwise it gets sold for scrap after ninety days."

"It...it's Angelo's car."

"Yes, sir, I understand."

"When will they be released from the hospital? Doctor said to talk to you."

"I imagine they will be released from the hospital in a few days. However, they are under arrest and will be detained until some matters can be investigated further."

"Arrested? Matters? What matters?" Vinny pulled the shot glass up to his lips.

"Both men are felons and there were loaded weapons found in the car. They will be arraigned on illegal weapons possession. You might want to think about getting council for your two employees."

"I don't know about no guns." Vinny put the shot glass down. His hand trembled.

"You don't know their destination?"

"No, sir. They were on their own."

"Uh-huh." Captain Kohler sighed. "I'll give the hospital permission to have them call you later today."

"I...I appreciate that. Yes, I'd like to talk to them."

"Very good, sir." The call ended.

—

The southeast corner of Montana was the ancient country of the Crow Indians. Many signs directed the traveler to sacred sites and battlegrounds. Lillian pointed to the sign for the Little Bighorn River and Custer's last battle.

"Oh, look, the Little Bighorn."

"I was reading about this area before I left home. Even as a kid, I was interested in the American Indian cultures, read all I could about it."

"Not much left, is there?" she asked, pensively.

"Not really. I read where it was pressure from the white settlers farther east that pushed the Sioux and Cheyenne into this area with the ensuing inter-tribal warfare. The Crow used to live here. I guess the Sioux came to dominate it later."

"It was the Sioux who fought Custer, wasn't it?" she asked.

"Yes, but I think other tribes had joined them. By then the buffalo herds had been decimated and the natives were starving. Then the railroads came along with more settlers."

"Where did the Indians go?"

"The few that survived went onto reservations or escaped into the wilds of Canada," Bob responded.

The high-plains awakened to spring with new grasses and flowers. Far-flung ranches and farms dotted the landscape. These family-owned businesses were the essence of life in this corner of the west. The pick-up truck, dusty boots and broad-rimmed hat were the trademarks of the working cowboy, and Bob had to smile when he thought of the shiny 4-wheel drive vehicles in the east that never left the paved road, and spent much of their life driving through the car wash.

I-90 crossed the Bighorn River and then the Yellowstone River to arrive at the city of Billings, surrounded by rim-rock, sandstone cliffs hundreds of feet high, and the green Yellowstone Valley beyond. Several snow capped mountain ranges was a great contrast to the lush farmland in the valley.

Bob signaled for a turn and exited I-90 to stop at a small shopping mall where the ubiquitous Burger King sign stood high.

"We made it to Montana," said Bob looking at Lillian as he got out of the truck.

She smiled as he came around to meet her, and silently took his arm.

They took their lunch to a table looking out on the parking lot and the camper.

"Looking at the map before…the road ahead is going to go through some spectacular country."

Lillian hesitated before replying. "If it weren't for these circumstances, there'd be so much to enjoy. I can't help but wonder what on earth we're going to do?"

"I keep thinking about it, but there doesn't seem to be many choices. If you were to mail the CD and record book back to them, I guess they would still come after you, huh?"

"Yes. I'm sure of it. I think they would fear what I might say to the FBI as much as anything else."

"Well, there *is* the FBI," he suggested.

She shook her head.

Bob continued. "If you walked into the FBI office and handed them the CD and book, they'd have to protect you since they'd want you as a material witness to testify against them."

Lillian shook her head again and looked at him. "I can't. I would never live to testify. Even with Joey and Vinny in jail, the family would send someone to locate me and silence me. It's done that way all the time. You read about it in the paper every time one of these trials comes up. They would probably go after Vinny and Joey as well. The family *will* protect itself."

"Can't you send the stuff to Joey's boss?" asked Bob.

"I could, but those two would still come after me. If they were dead, then I would send it to Joey's boss. I could risk it then."

"Who is this guy, Joey's boss?"

Lillian toyed with her food. "Joey's a capo and reports to Mike Santos, under-boss to Frank Cappella. Frank is head of one of the families in Chicago."

"Do you know these guys?"

"Not really. I've heard that Santos used to be a top enforcer, but he's been moved to some sort of management position for Cappella. I'm sure that Cappella can be a deadly man to cross, but when I was introduced and saw him at the house, I didn't get the scary feeling like with some of the others. Cappella was always respectful to me." She looked away for a moment before continuing. "They look like your average businessmen, well groomed, nice clothes. After a while, Joey didn't take me anywhere, kept me at home, so I didn't see much of them."

"Could you get to these guys? Give them the stuff, explain it to them?" asked Bob.

"I don't know what Joey has told them. If I had to do this in person, Joey would kill me before I could say anything. He'd feign some excuse, even in front of Cappella. He'd have to. What choice would he have?"

They sat silently for a few minutes. Finishing their meal, Lillian looked out the window, the long gaze that Bob had come to recognize.

"What are you thinking?" he asked.

She shook her head, bit her lip, and then turned to look at him. "I saw that you switched to buying gas with cash. I'm glad, otherwise they could track you through your credit card."

"Yeah, I didn't want to make it easy for them. When we get to the ranch, we can lay low for a while and figure out a workable plan."

"They can find out where people's relatives live in a few minutes on the Internet. I've seen them do it. Joey's got some ace computer kid that he uses. The kid's still in high school. There's no escaping them if they really want to find someone." She looked out the window. "I'm afraid. I don't want anything to happen to you. You've been nothing but kind to me."

"Lillian, I…"

"They could find out that you have relatives in Montana, and know exactly where to locate them. It wouldn't take them long to figure it out." She turned to face him, tears in her eyes. "I can't do this to you."

"We beat off two of them. It's not going to be easy for them now, so far away from home."

He didn't want her to leave, to go out of his life. A sense of foreboding crept into his thoughts. How could he keep her with him?

"The two goons weren't real shooters, must have been some guys they had available on short notice. Next time they'll send a hit man out on a plane. We wouldn't see it coming. I *know* Joey and Vinny have done this before. They've gotten rid of rats and double crossers this way. They're just found dead. Nobody knows - *nobody . . . cares*. That's why they're so desperate now;

they fear the same will happen to *them*. They want the CD and record book, and want me dead. God, I should have never taken it – so stupid of me."

"Where can you hide from them? You said they'd find you," said Bob anxiously.

"I have friends in Salt Lake. They could find me a place to hide for a while, without putting themselves in danger. They're pretty resourceful people, knew them in Chicago. I met them through church"

"But doesn't Joey know about them?"

"I'm sure he's seen them around. But they've been away from Chicago for several years. I've been to church functions with them, got rather close to them. Joey might recall them…maybe."

She hesitated before continuing. "I want to take a bus from Butte to Salt Lake City. There's got to be at least one a day going there." She looked with imploring eyes at Bob and saw the sadness in his face. "Bob? Please?"

"Of course, if you want to," Bob said. "But I really think it would be safer for you if you stayed with me for a while."

Lillian looked at him. "You are a good man. I can't bear to think of anything happening to you. Hopefully, they'll leave you alone when they realize that I'm not with you."

"I think those gangsters would come after me anyway, try to get me to tell them where you are."

She hesitated, her lip trembled. "I have to go. Please."

Bob nodded slowly.

—

Vinny waited in the back office of the Playpen. He took a gulp of his bourbon and realized his hands were shaking. He sat the tumbler back on the table. The doors from the club burst open and Joey barged in, unmindful of the door slamming into a waitress.

Vinny was fearful of Joey's rages, his stomach knotted. He didn't meet Joey's gaze. Joey sat down and brought his fist down hard on the table. Vinny's bourbon glass skidded away from him. He reached for it.

"Goddamn you, Vinny! What the hell happened?"

"Like I said on the phone, they got in this accident. They were trying to get the camper to stop. They shot at them, but they wouldn't stop. They were getting ready to take out the driver when truck ran them off the road."

Joey could barely contain his anger as he heard about Angelo and Lou. "What? You shitting me?"

"Joey, they were good guys. They did a lot of jobs, don't know what happened." Vinny's voice trembled.

Joey roared. "You don't know what happened? What are you saying? That some old fart took out a couple of our guys?"

Vinny tried to keep calm. "Angelo called me. Both are in a Sioux Falls hospital. The car is wrecked. They said a truck pushed them off the road. The police arrested them, but they didn't tell them anything."

"Arrested them? What?" Joey stared at Vinny.

"They found guns in the car," Vinny stammered. "They...they're gonna be arraigned next week."

"Un-fuckin' believable!" Joey's fist came down hard on the table. "We lost over two days! We're both dead if we don't get this job done, and quick!"

"A couple of our guys are over in Sioux Falls right now. They just finished a piece of work and are hanging out with some friends. I could call them, get them up to speed on this, and have them do the job."

"What kind of guys?" Joey scowled. He sounded dubious.

"They're good at making people disappear. That's their thing."

"This better not be another pair of Keystone Cops or it'll be all over for us."

"Joey, I..."

Joey interrupted, getting up and bending over the table into Vinny's face. "This is on you Vinny. When this is over, we're going to square this up."

—

Fred pushed the big rig along at 80 mph, frustrated at losing nearly a whole day at the warehouse in Minneapolis. Someone had been suspicious of what appeared to them as new seals on the trailer doors. A complete inventory had been ordered before he was allowed to get underway with a load for delivery in Seattle. Of course, they hadn't found any discrepancies. He pushed hard to make up the time. There's no bonus if he arrives late. Then as he entered Wyoming, the phone call changed his plans.

The dispatcher in Minneapolis advised him to be on the lookout for a maroon Dodge truck with a cab-over camper and Massachusetts plates. No explanation was offered and Fred knew better than to ask. The dispatcher gave him a new route, one that would add a day to his travel. When Fred asked about the delivery bonus, the dispatcher assured him that a bonus would still be his, and more, if he spotted and reported the camper truck. There would be other truckers looking for this vehicle, and all main routes through Montana, Idaho and Washington were being covered. Fred was cautioned to be vigilant, particularly at rest stops and towns. He glanced at the map, Billings was two hours ahead on I-90, and then he'd go through Bozeman and into Butte. His assigned detour would take him over a slow moving state road, route 43. He'd pass through the town of Camden before turning north onto US-93 toward Missoula. He wondered, why all the effort for some tourist camper? "What the hell, as long as they're paying…"

———

Lillian and Bob picked up their coffee cups and left the Burger King. Neither said much, awed by the scenery as they drove west on I-90 for hours. The landscape changed as mountain ranges rose from the horizon. The high plains were left behind. The Absaroka Range dominated the southern vista. Snow still lay deep in the high ravines on these mountains. Dense stands of conifers covered much of the slopes. I-90 followed the Yellowstone River into the town of Livingston. An hour later the town of Bozeman, surrounded by lofty mountains, came into view. Bozeman sat at the foot of Gallatin Valley with the Gallatin and Madison Mountains to the south and the Bridger Range to the northeast. Lillian looked around at the dramatic landscape unfolding.

She broke a long silence. "This is so beautiful. I've never seen anything like this."

"Me neither. I am so glad that I decided to make this trip."

"I'm glad that you did, too." She reached over and clasped his arm. "It will be hard for me to leave you."

"For me, too." Bob glanced at her. He feared that a mob shooter would find her. He knew too, that he didn't want to lose her company and the friendship that had become important to him. He liked the warmth of her hand on his arm. He liked a lot of things about her.

"I wish things could be different," he said.

The dark conifer-covered slopes gave way to aspen at the lower levels, now bursting with new green of spring. Snow melt swelled the streams into rushing torrents, tumbling over boulders, downhill toward the Gallatin and Madison Rivers and farther, to form the mighty Missouri. They rolled the windows down to allow the cool clean air to swirl around them.

"Look at this, so beautiful," she exclaimed, her eyes darting from window to window.

"The air is so clean. You can see forever," said Bob inhaling deeply.

"We've crossed the continental divide, saw the sign."

"Yep, we're in the Pacific watershed now," Bob added.

Their conversation quieted again until early evening when as they approached the Montana Avenue exit. Each knew what lay ahead. Bob turned off I-90 and drove north into downtown Butte until he reached Broadway. He then followed the signs to the bus terminal and found a parking spot close to the building.

Lillian reached for the door handle. "Bob, I want to do this alone… please. I'll be right back." Her eyes begged him for understanding.

He nodded. His heart pounded. Bob saw the tears in her eyes, felt them well up in his and bit his lip. She got out of the truck and disappeared behind him into the building. He hardly noticed the old historic buildings of downtown. He thought of her, of her disappearing forever from his life. He couldn't accept that she would be safe with friends elsewhere, not if Vinny and Joey were as evil and determined as they seemed. She had said it herself; the mob can get to anyone and they would eventually find her. Fear clutched at his stomach.

Lillian finally returned, opened the door, and climbed into the truck, ticket in hand. She looked at Bob. "The bus leaves at 7:30. Do you want to get something to eat?"

He nodded. "Okay."

"The ticket man said that there was a good place a few blocks east of here. It's called the Uptown Café. It's right on Broadway."

"I guess I'll just leave the truck here instead of looking for another parking place."

She nodded, "It should be okay. Let's walk." She got out of the truck.

He came around the truck and made sure the doors were locked before they started toward the restaurant. They didn't say anything, and when he glanced at her he saw tears on her cheek. She tried to look away. He stopped and then gently pulled her into a doorway, holding her as she sobbed. His heart went out to her. He couldn't know the agony that she felt, but knew that he ached to think that she would soon be gone. He kissed her wet face and then found her mouth. She returned his kiss hungrily, her arms encircled his neck. Then she pulled away, and padded her eyes with the back of her hand.

"I just hope you'll be safe," said Bob with a catch in his throat.

She nodded, grabbed Bob's arm, and pulled him along to the doorway of the Uptown Café. While they waited a few minutes for seating, Lillian excused herself and went into the ladies' restroom. By the time she returned, her makeup was again immaculate. He smiled at her and she melted gently into his arms. Neither said anything.

The hostess seated them and presented the menu. She recommended a pasta dish, the special for that day. They both ordered it. Bob asked for a carafe of wine. They were silent until it arrived and Bob poured the two glasses.

"Did you talk to your friends? The people in Salt Lake City."

"No. I was afraid to call." She stopped and kept her eyes on her wineglass.

"Do you think someone might be listening in on them already?"

She shook her head and then looked at him. "I don't know what to think. I thought I'd just go there and get a hotel room and then approach them. They'll help me, I'm sure."

"But you're afraid," Bob stated.

There was a pause before Lillian replied. "I keep wondering if I'm bringing trouble to them. Do I have any right to do that?"

"Can they handle trouble, if it comes?"

"Bill and Sandy are just regular people. He's an accountant. She's home with a nine year old boy."

"It's difficult to hide without getting a real change of identity."

"That's what the FBI wanted me to do. Joey got wind of it. He's probably thinking about it right now." She shook her head and bit on her lip.

The waitress arrived with their supper. They tried to focus on the food to change the mood. Lillian smiled at her dish. "Looks wonderful."

Conversation during supper was sparse; sadness had a grip on both of them. Lillian glanced at Bob from time to time. What was he thinking, she wondered? The attachment she felt for him had happened so subtly. She didn't want to leave him, but she couldn't endanger him any more. He had been so kind to her, so unselfish. It would be unbearable if anything happened to him. But it would be painful to leave him, never see him again.

Bob interrupted her thoughts. "What time do you get into Salt Lake?"

"Bus is scheduled to arrive at 3:30 in the morning, an ungodly hour." She forced a grin. "I'll get a hotel room, sleep awhile before I try to contact my friends."

"Lillian, I have a cell phone in my truck. I'll turn it on later, keep it on, so if you run into a problem you can call me."

She saw the seriousness in his face and tears welled up in her eyes. She watched as he wrote the phone number down on a napkin.

"Please, put this in your purse," he said as he handed it to her.

She took the napkin and opened her facial compact, tore the napkin and inserted the phone number behind the mirror. "I won't lose it. Thank you."

The waitress dropped off the check and Bob put the payment in the check holder. He got up and pulled out Lillian's chair. Her hair brushed his face and he smelled her perfume as she stood up. He softly caressed her arm. She turned and looked at him curiously as they started toward the front of the restaurant. He met her gaze and smiled. Her eyes lingered on his face for a moment, before she looked down in time to avoid bumping into a table. The sun was well down when they came outside.

"If you want to drive some more today, I'll be okay here. It's only an hour more until the bus leaves." She glanced at him briefly.

"8:00?"

"Yes. I better get my stuff out of the camper."

As they approached the bus station, Bob stopped and with his hand on her arm, guided her close to him. She looked at him, sorrow in her eyes.

"Lillian, don't go." He couldn't keep the tremor out of his voice.

"I have to. I…" She came into his arms, hiding her face against his chest.

"Don't go." He was just barely able to whisper it. His heart pounded. He held her firmly.

"I don't want to leave you, but I have to." Her arms encircled him, her face pressed against him.

"No. Stay with me. I don't want to lose you. You're very special to me."

"Bob…" She held tightly to him.

He felt her trembling. "Stay with me; don't go."

She looked up at him, tears wet her face. Her lips trembled.

He covered her mouth with his as her arms encircled his neck.

"I don't want to leave you." She found his mouth again, hungrily kissing his lips, his face. "I want to be with you."

"Stay with me. Be with me tonight," he whispered.

"Yes, I want to." She kissed him tenderly. "I'll return my ticket, be just a minute." Lillian hurried into the bus station.

"They gave me my money back." She smiled and put her arm through his. "Oh Bob, I *do* want to be with you."

"We're going to solve this problem, this Vinny and Joey thing." Bob said with as much conviction as he could muster.

She squeezed his arm as they came up to the truck. "Yes, we will."

He opened the door and she took her seat. She ran her fingers across his face, looking into his eyes. "I love you, Bob."

He smiled, "We'll be okay."

She nodded, "Yes."

He went around the truck to his door. His heart pounded.

They topped a hill and left Butte behind. Bob saw the big sign for the Hilltop Motel and the Conoco Truck Stop and decided that it would be wise to top off the tank. He left the highway and turned onto the access road to the Conoco station. The place was crowded with motor homes at the gas pumps and a double line of trailer trucks at the diesel stands. Bob started the pump and went to clean the windows. He looked in at Lillian. She was lovely he thought; and there was something else, an inner beauty that he saw from time to time, a youthful softness that hadn't been scarred by her years of turmoil. Yes, she was special. He turned to the fuel pump when he heard it click off. The sun was below the horizon; he wouldn't drive too much farther, maybe another hour, he thought. He got into the truck and closed the door. When he was about to turn the ignition key, she placed her hand on his. He looked at her.

"Let's stay here at the motel. I want to be with you tonight." Her eyes held his.

He pulled her towards him, holding her, kissing her. A horn sounded behind him. Startled, they both laughed. He started the engine and moved away from the pumps, behind the truck stop to the Hillside Motel.

Hearing the bathroom door open, he turned to look at her. She was wrapped in a bath towel. The small lamp on the nightstand cast her in a soft glow. A few feet away, she let the towel slip to the floor.

"I left my nightie in the camper," she said softly.

He reached his hand toward her. "You are beautiful."

He pulled back the blanket and she entered his embrace. They clung to each other, the heat stirring. He tasted the tears on her face.

"Lillian…?"

She looked at him. "I'm so happy to be with you."

CHAPTER 9 TIMBERLINE RANCH

They stopped at the Conoco truck stop for breakfast. Neither had wanted to get out of bed, savoring the closeness and comfort. They found a booth by the window overlooking the fueling area. Bob raised his coffee cup to his lips, sipped slowly and looked at her. Lillian stared at the traffic going by the fuel pumps.

"What are you thinking?" he asked. Sadness had come over her face, a look that he knew all too well.

She reached for his hand, squeezed it and looked at him, but didn't say anything.

"How long do you think we have before they come?" said Bob.

She shrugged, "Vinny and Joey, they're both crazy. And now they have to be worried about the big man finding out what they've been up to, all the skimming they've done. I know they want me dead."

"That's not going to happen."

She looked into his eyes; a warm glow came into her face. "I love you, Bob."

"Excuse me, may I take your order?" asked a cheerful young woman.

Bob folded the Montana map so that he could see the area west of Butte. They got back onto I-90, heading toward the town of Anaconda. There they found state route 374 heading west to the small town of Windon, in the valley of the Big Hole River. Forested mountains rose on both sides.

"I'm stopping for pictures here and there," said Bob. "I don't know when I'll be by here again."

Lillian nodded. "I just worry about them catching up to us." She turned to glance out the back window.

"They'd have to be awfully lucky to know we turned off of I-90 here," said Bob as he stopped the truck.

The beauty and ruggedness of the land left them in awe. He read aloud some of the historical notes of the Indian wars in the northern Rockies from the Montana Handbook he had purchased a few months earlier.

Lillian listened attentively. "I guess I never really thought much about the American Indians out here, other than the version given in school books."

"Me neither."

It was midmorning when they arrived in Windon. The little crossroads town boasted several bars and restaurants, and a motel and grocery. Lillian pointed out an art gallery.

"Didn't expect to see that," she exclaimed.

"Life is changing here too," he said.

Bob looked at the notes he had made from the instructions his cousin Ralph had given him. He spotted route 443 on the map and the towns of Camden and Randolph up against the Bitterroot Mountains. He would call Ralph when he got to Camden and get the directions to Timberline Ranch. They departed Windon and soon came upon the monument marking the fierce Nez Perce battle with the US Cavalry in 1877. They got out of the truck and looked at the plaque and took photos of each other.

Just before noon, they drove into the town of Camden. It wasn't a large town, Bob thought, only about 20,000 according to the map. There were several traffic lights in the business district where he spotted the courthouse and sheriff's office. Nearby were an old hotel and two department stores. Numerous bars and restaurants lined the street.

Bob looked over at Lillian. "I have to call Ralph, but first should we get some lunch?"

"That would be great. I see a Chili's up ahead." She smiled and pointed.

"Is that what you want? We could do something more upscale if you like."

"I like Chili's. Is it okay?"

"Sure," he said and her face lit up in a smile. It pleased him to see her happy.

—

The big rig came to a stop at the curb just before the parking lot. There was a release of air and then the engine stopped. Fred climbed down from the cab, stretched and yawned. He liked Chili's and thought about a large pork BBQ sandwich. Part way across the parking lot to the entrance, he stopped, staring toward the rear of the lot where a maroon truck camper was parked. He started walking again, changing course to enter from the door closest to the back of the building. As he came closer, he saw the Massachusetts license plate. "Holy shit! That's them. Gotta be them," he said under his breath while he reached for his cell phone. He leaned against a newspaper box and punched in the number for his dispatcher.

"R and R Trucking, Evelyn speaking."

"Yes, hello. This is Fred Bucari. I'm calling from Camden, Montana, about the notice for a certain camper truck."

"Just a moment, Fred. I'll connect you with my supervisor."

The line went quiet. Fred thought about the extra bonus this find would net.

"Fred, this is Bill Paglino," said a calm, low key voice. "You have something for me?"

"Yes, sir. I'm looking at a maroon Dodge truck with Mass. plates and a cab-over camper."

"You're where? Camden? Where's that?"

"West of Butte, off route 43. It's on one of the routes dispatch gave me earlier."

"Okay. I got it now on my map. Do you see anyone in it or nearby?" The voice was calm and measured. Fred already didn't like him. *Nasty prick*, he thought.

"No, sir. I'm outside of Chili's and there are lots of people inside. I don't know yet who goes with the camper."

"Okay. Go on inside, order something. See if you can spot who leaves and gets into the camper. Then call me back and tell me the direction they head. Be ready to spot that."

"Okay. When I spot them, I'll call you, and then continue my route."

"Yes. That's fine. You got yourself a bonus."

Fred closed his cell phone and smiled.

—

Bob brought the tray with their lunch to the window booth where Lillian sat. He saw for a moment the faraway look in her eyes, the long stare out of the window.

"We'll be okay. They'll probably forget about us soon, way out here."

She smiled wistfully. "I wish that were true. This place is so lovely."

"Who'd think to look for us here?" Bob raised an eyebrow.

"Oh Bob, when I was doing stuff for Joey, he showed me how he could find anybody, illegally of course, by following credit card transactions, breaking into the DMV computer for address changes, checking with Social Security, and he even had someone in Bank of America he paid to feed him information."

"I haven't been using my credit card for awhile, just cash," Bob commented.

"That will slow them down. The credit card companies were easy marks. He had some whiz-kid outa high school cracking the passwords into credit card companies. They'll eventually find out you have relatives out here, it won't be that hard."

"Once we get to the ranch, it'll be difficult for them to get to you. They may give up." Bob tried to sound optimistic.

"Joey and Vinny won't give up. They're afraid of what I know and what is on that disc and the record book. If their bosses ever find out about all the skimming that they've been doing…well, they'd be worse off than us. No, they'll keep looking for me, for us. They'll want to find us as soon as they can. They are probably running pretty scared right now."

"How come they didn't send out a high powered shooter right away?" asked Bob.

"They'd have to ask their boss, Santos, for permission. I'm sure Cappella would hear about it. They couldn't risk having the higher ups knowing."

They fell silent, both working on their lunch. Bob got up and brought back more coffee. Lillian looked up as he slid into the booth.

"I'm sorry. I'm just frightened."

"He put his hand over hers. "I know. We'll be alright though."

"I love you, Bob." Her eyes glistened.

"I love you, too."

In the truck, Bob reached for his cell-phone in the glove box. In his small notebook he found Ralph's phone number. After three rings, someone picked it up.

"Ralph? It's your cousin Bob."

"Hey, Bob. Where are you? I was thinking you'd be showing up one of these days."

"I'm in Camden. We just had lunch at Chili's."

"We? What we? I thought you were alone." Ralph sounded confused.

"It's a long story. Her name is Lillian, a very special friend."

"You old rascal! Get over here and tell me all about it."

"Yeah, that's why I called. I need directions."

"Okay. When you leave Chili's, turn right. After a few miles you'll come to the town of Randolph, mostly bars. A few more miles, you'll be in Elk Creek."

"That sounds easy enough. Where's the ranch?" asked Bob.

"Go through Elk Creek, three more miles. It is on your right, you can't miss it. You'll see the big gate and sign over it."

"You sure we won't be a bother?"

Ralph laughed. "Oh, for crissake, get over here. It's been a long time."

"Thanks. We're on our way."

"Here's the gate," Bob said. "This is a six mile dirt road to the ranch buildings. We'll just take it slow, looks kinda bumpy."

"Six miles? Wow. I've never seen so much space."

Bob got out of the truck to open the ranch gate. Lillian drove through and Bob closed it again. He got back in the truck as Lillian slid back over to the passenger side.

"This is beautiful country, so open and wild."

"I was thinking the same thing. The fellow that owns this place is Tom Bauer. He lives here with his wife and small child. I think I told you already."

"Yes, I remember. What's his wife's name?"

"Tom's wife? Karen. Ralph is the foreman and he has his own cabin. He lives there with his wife, Susan."

"They have a daughter, too?"

"Yes. Liz is in college, but may be home now for the summer."

"Are you nervous?"

He hesitated a moment before replying. "I guess I am. I don't want to be a bother."

"I'll take my cues from you, okay?"

"Sure. I guess we'll play it by ear."

—

A small charter jet arrived from Sioux Falls, landing at the Camden airport, and taxied to the terminal, the last flight of the day. Two men stepped onto the tarmac. The copilot pulled the two suitcases from the cargo area and set them on the ground. "Have a good trip, guys. Give us 24 hours heads-up before you need us here again."

"Will do," said Jay Bono.

Jay and Ron Novak picked up their bags and quickly entered the terminal.

Jay looked about. "Place is deserted. Supposed to be some guy around here with the keys for the car."

"Here comes some dude, down at the far end." Ron pointed to a large man waddling toward them. They moved quickly toward him.

"You the two guys lookin' for a car?" A cold cigar stump bobbed on his lips.

"Yeah. Supposed to be a large car here for us," offered Jay.

The big man reached into his overalls and pulled out a sheaf of papers with his greasy hands. "What's the name on the order?" He squinted at the small text.

"Bono. Jay Bono."

"Yeah. That's what it says here. Best we have right now is a Taurus sedan."

"Freaking Taurus?" said Ron.

"We'll take it," said Jay shaking his head.

"Slap your signature on here and it's all yours." He handed the papers to Jay, who signed the form and returned all but the customer copy.

"Here's the keys. It's a gray Taurus parked at the end of the building. Tank's full. Make sure you fill it when you return. Gimme a call before you head back, make sure I'm here."

"Yeah, got it. Thanks," said Jay. He picked up his bag, and he and Ron headed for the far doorway.

"What a hayseed. I can still smell that stogie," quipped Ron, a brief look over his shoulder.

Jay chuckled. "This ain't Chicago." He pointed to the glass doors. "I see the car."

"Best there is here? A Taurus?" Ron shook his head.

"I'm not looking to stand out, have these hicks stare at us, remember us," said Jay.

"But a Taurus?"

"Shut up. That's all they had."

They pushed open the doors and in a few steps were at the car. They tossed their bags into the trunk.

"Okay. Now if the hotel room is reserved we'll get some sleep," said Jay. "We'll get the lay of the place in the morning."

"We're supposed to find these guys in the camper truck? Vinny didn't give us much to go on," said Ron.

Jay nodded in agreement. "Trucker spotted them in this town. Vinny had someone searching the Internet and found out there was another Stehling in this telephone area code, living at this Timberline Ranch. We'll check it out tomorrow."

"How we gonna find this ranch?" asked Ron.

"All I know, it's some miles south of here. Some town called Elk Creek."

"Can't imagine living out here," mumbled Ron.

"Yeah, wouldn't be me." Jay started the car. "Let's get some sleep."

—

Bob approached the ranch buildings slowly and parked in front of the barn. Ralph, sitting on a fence rail, had watched them come up the road. Now he jumped down and walked towards them, a big smile on his face. He reached for the passenger door and opened it.

"Welcome to Timberline, folks!" He gave a quick appreciative glance at Lillian and then looked over at Bob. "You old scoundrel."

Bob ignored the quip. "It sure is good to see you. Ralph, this is Lillian."

"Well come on, get down outa there, both of you. We're glad to have you."

Bob came around the back of the camper and stood by Lillian's side, shook hands with Ralph.

"We don't want to impose on you or on the ranch. I did want to see you though," Bob said hesitantly as he searched Ralph's face.

"Oh, for crying out loud, we were looking forward to your arrival. Tom knows you're coming, no problem at all. We have riding guests here, sure. You'll get to meet them later."

"Ralph, this place is so lovely," exclaimed Lillian.

"It is. I wouldn't live anywhere else."

Ralph showed them the lodge and introduced them to a few of the guests who were staying that week. Bob and Lillian looked appreciatively at the lodge, a building of large cedar logs and stone. They met the kitchen staff, and then Ralph suggested that they walk over to the Bauer cabin and meet Tom and his family. Smiles and well wishes from some of the ranch guests followed them to the door.

Ralph knocked and the door was opened immediately. Tom's warm smile and graciousness soon put Bob and Lillian at ease. His wife, Karen, with a small child in hand, entered the living room and introductions were made. Caitlyn, barely two years old, hid behind her mother and peered guardedly around her legs.

Tom looked at Ralph. "How about we set them up in cabin 3. It will be empty this week."

Ralph nodded. "That would be great; number 3 it is."

"Say, better introduce Bandit to them." He winked at Ralph.

Outside on the porch, Tom whistled shrilly. Bob and Lillian looked around. A few seconds elapsed, and suddenly a huge dog came tearing up the path.

"Bandit, sit," commanded Tom as the dog came up to them.

The dog sat obediently, tongue hanging out.

"Bandit, meet the new guests. Go on, just pet him. I want him to know who you are."

Bob stroked the dog and rubbed his neck. "Wow, he's a big boy."

Lillian petted him and he nuzzled her, as if asking for more. She petted him again.

"He's part wolf," Tom said, "but a really good friend. He'll be your friend too, now that he knows you."

"He's gorgeous," said Lillian as she reached to pet him again.

Tom turned to them. "I'm glad that you could come. Ralph's been talking about your visit. Please feel at home here. I have to get over to my guests in the lodge, but Ralph will look after you." He stepped off the porch and headed for the lodge.

Ralph looked at Bob. "Why don't you bring your camper over to my cabin? Need to keep it out of the way of the horses and horse trailers. I'm just down here a few hundred feet. Go on, I'll be talking to Lillian while you do that." Ralph grinned. "We'll head down that way."

Bob started toward the barn where he had left his truck. Ralph rubbed his chin and turned toward Lillian with a sly grin.

"I guess Bob told you about us here at the ranch, but he hasn't told *me* anything about *you*. Last time we talked, he was driving out here by himself. He's full of surprises."

"It's a long story." She glanced at him. "We met in Illinois. I was in a spot of trouble and he helped, probably saved my life."

They heard Bob coming with the truck and moved aside to let him pass. Ralph pointed to the far side of the cabin where there was a graveled parking spot.

"I gotta hear the whole story. But don't get me wrong; I am very happy for you and Bob."

"Thank you. I care a lot about him." She met his gaze; he was smiling. Bob walked up to them.

"Come on in you two. Meet the girls."

"You remember my wife Susan? And of course, Liz is a bit bigger than you remember."

Liz looked at Bob shyly.

"Bigger and lovelier, I'd say." Bob smiled as Liz blushed.

Susan came up to Bob and hugged him. "It sure has been a while. Vegas, wasn't it? You look great."

Bob turned, "I'd like you to meet my friend, Lillian."

Susan gave Lillian a hug. "I'm dying to hear the your story," she said with a curious smile. Turning to Bob, "You're full of surprises."

He put his arm around Lillian's waist. "No more surprised than we are."

"Ralph, why don't you show them around, while Liz and I finish up here? Tom asked us to join him in the lodge for supper with the other guests." Susan kissed Ralph dismissively on the cheek and turned to the kitchen with Liz.

The three of them stood by the railing looking out on the broad pasture where groups of Angus cattle grazed some distance away. Horses nickered in the corral behind them. On the road a group of guest riders were heading back to the ranch, a dust cloud rising up behind them. Soon all the riders would be in, Ralph informed them, and the wranglers would make sure that the horses received feed, water and a rubdown.

"We treat our horses well," said Ralph, "give them get the best of care. They're trained at a ranch in Wyoming, where we keep most of them over the winter."

"But you need to know how to ride – don't you?" asked Lillian.

"We get guests that never been on a horse and in a couple days they're on some short trail rides. These horses are trained to be very tolerant. But of course, they expect some measure of respect," replied Ralph. "With those few folks that have problems, it is usually lack of understanding, and we work with them."

Bob turned. "Does the guest pick out a horse? How's that work?"

Ralph shook his head. "No. We match the horse to the guest's size, weight and experience. The assigned horse belongs to the guest for the length of their stay. It is up to them to take care of it, brush it, feed it, and water it. Of course, sometimes we get some lazy people and one of the wranglers ends up taking care of the horse."

"Do you get many guests that just come here to hang out?' asked Lillian.

"Not many, but we do get a few that just want to hike and clear their minds."

Ralph turned toward Bob, running his hand over his chin then grinned. "You'll have to pardon me, but I'm really curious about how you two met."

Bob looked at Lillian. She nodded subtly. "It's a long story, but briefly, we met at a diner in Illinois. Lillian was working there. There was some trouble with her boss, and I helped her get away."

Ralph looked at them and shook his head. "I bet there's more to it than that."

"Well, we had some trouble on the way out here," said Bob with a glance at Lillian.

"Holy cow! You'll have to tell us later, over dinner, okay?" said Ralph getting off the fence rail. "Right now we should get cleaned up. I'll show you where the washer and dryer are. Supper is in the lodge at 6:30."

They walked back towards the lodge and cabins. "The guest cabins have their own showers; these are for anyone to use. It's best to use the laundry after 2 p.m., that way the housekeeping staff can get their work done on time."

"Thanks Ralph, we sure could stand to do some washing," said Bob.

"Also, there's an iron in there and the board hangs on the wall." Then he added, "I'll see you at the lodge for supper. Wine and hors d'oeuvres at 6, if you're interested."

Lillian waved, "See you then and thanks."

They brought their clothes into the cabin and laid them out on the bed. Lillian shook her head. "I hope this supper isn't too fancy. I don't have much to wear."

"I have clean jeans and shirt. They're practically new." Bob scratched his chin, as he looked over their clothes.

"I could wear jeans, I have a clean pair," mused Lillian. "This white blouse would look good, don't you think?"

"Yes, wear that. I think it would be nice. Are you going to let your hair down?"

"Oh, should I brush it out?" She looked at him with a teasing smile.

He nodded and stepped toward her. She came into his arms, turning her face upward. He kissed her and held her tightly for a few seconds.

"This is so wonderful…too good to be true." said Lillian.

Lillian and Bob entered the lodge at 6:30. Ralph and Tom were mixing with the guests and introductions were quickly made. In a few minutes, the conversation was back to a spirited discussion of the day's horseback riding, leaving Bob feeling at loose ends. He felt Lillian put her arm through his and he looked at her.

"I don't ever want to lose you."

She turned her head up and kissed his cheek.

Tom appeared by their side. "I'm glad you could join us."

Lillian remarked, "Wasn't sure if we had anything to wear."

"This is a ranch. Just be comfortable," said Tom.

Bob turned to Tom. "We appreciate your hospitality. Ralph talked about the ranch on the phone, but seeing it and being here; well, it is wonderful."

Tom looked from Bob to Lillian. "Now you can tell us how you got here."

Lillian replied, "Sure, we can talk about our trip out here." Her grip tightened on Bob's arm.

"Come on, the cook is about ready to ring the supper bell. Let's find us a seat," urged Ralph.

Lillian turned to Tom. "Are your wife and Caitlyn joining us?"

"Not today. Karen has her hands full. She helps me in the office every day, and our daughter has a lot of energy."

Tom sat them next to him near the head of the table. The cook beat on the dinner bell hanging by the back door; the notes loud enough to be heard throughout the ranch, bringing the guests and wranglers to supper.

The dozen guests, hungry from a day of riding in the cool air, launched into the meal with gusto. A pile of T-bone steaks and baked potatoes quickly disappeared as a few people went back for seconds. Several conversations were going on at one time, and it was Ralph and Susan near the far end of the big table who asked Bob if he would tell everyone about his trip from Massachusetts. Suddenly the table quieted and everyone turned toward Bob. He cleared his throat.

"Well…I'm retired and decided to leave Massachusetts, where I grew up, and see the rest of the country. I bought a pickup truck and a camper and headed west about a week ago."

"Hi, I'm Elaine. I'm curious; why did you want to leave home? Where was that?" the older lady asked.

"I lived in Lowell. It's north of Boston. I didn't feel about the area as I once did. The place changed so much the last twenty years, didn't feel the same anymore. Also, I've started to write and wanted to know what was out in the rest of the country. I wanted to see and feel things that I didn't know about. I thought that being on the road would be a good way to do it."

"Which way did you come out here?" asked the man sitting next to Elaine.

"I came out I-90. That's the Mass. Turnpike. I took it to Buffalo, down through Pennsylvania and into Ohio. I was on I-90 all the way through Ohio, Indiana and Illinois. The second day out I stopped at a diner in Rockford, Illinois. I heard on the CB that they served pretty good meals and I thought, why not?"

A young woman interrupted and asked, "Where did you meet Lillian?"

Bob smiled, "I'm just comin' to that." He paused for a few seconds. "Lillian was working in this diner, waited on me at the counter. We got to talking. She wanted out of there, crazy ex-husband, lousy job. When I finished supper, we both left."

"Get out! Just like that?" asked a fellow sitting by Ralph and Susan.

Bob saw Liz give him a look and then roll her eyes.

"Craziest thing either one of us ever did," added Bob. He looked at Lillian. "But I'm not sorry."

Lillian looked down the length of the table. "It was crazy, I guess. There was nothing for me there, though. When we talked, it just felt right. I grabbed a few things and we left."

Tom shook his head. "Amazing. Sounds like an old movie."

"Well, I guess you've had time to get to know each other pretty well," offered Elaine.

"We did a lot of talking...almost non-stop," replied Lillian.

"And then what?" asked Ralph.

"We poked along, stopped here and there, enjoyed our company," Bob replied. "We don't have any real plans. I wanted to visit my cousin here at the ranch before moving on to the coast. I have some friends in Washington and Oregon."

Lillian looked at Bob with glistening eyes. "We've kind of grown on each other."

Bob smiled. "Yes, indeed."

There was a clatter of raised glasses and words of encouragement. Soon the guests drifted away from the dining room, outside to walk or retire to their cabins. Tom and Ralph found their two guests on the front porch.

"That was a great meal. We really enjoyed it," said Lillian, turning to the two men.

Tom looked at Lillian and then to Ralph. "I'm pretty good at body language, and you two haven't even begun to tell us what really happened out there."

Ralph spoke. "Bob...maybe you didn't want to tell everyone, and that's fine, but you should tell us. We are your friends."

Bob looked at Lillian. She gave a slight nod and squeezed his arm. "You're right. I didn't want to talk about this in front of them. I really don't think we should involve you in this, it'll just bring trouble your way."

Tom shook his head. "Let's not worry about that. Suppose we get together in my office, shut the door, and we'll listen to what you have to say. Maybe we can be of some help."

Bob felt the squeeze on his arm. He nodded at the two men. "Okay."

Bob and Lillian followed Tom back to his office. He had mentioned to Ralph that Susan and Liz should also attend. As everyone entered the office, Tom went around quickly removing stacks of papers and pamphlets from the chairs and invited everyone to sit. Liz found a comfortable spot on the floor.

Tom cleared his throat. "Tell us how you met and what the circumstances were, and what happened on the way out. Everything you say stays with us, no one else."

Bob cleared his throat. "I heard about the Lawndale Diner in Rockford from chatter on the CB. I thought I'd check it out. Lillian was working there, waited on me at the counter. After she took my order and was in the kitchen, I heard a commotion and loud voices and things dropping. It sounded like a fight." Bob looked at Lillian and continued. "I thought I heard a woman cry out. Anyway, I went back there. The cook seemed to be in a rage about something and Lillian and the dishwasher kid were catching the brunt of this guy's anger. When I saw him make a move toward Lillian with a mallet, I decked him with a bottle."

"Ouch! Didn't kill him?" asked Ralph.

"No, knocked him out for a while. I asked Lillian if she wanted to get out of there. She went to get some of her things from the upstairs apartment and beat it out the back door. I convinced the dishwasher kid to get out before the jerk on the floor woke up."

"I don't guess you got any dinner that night," said Ralph laughing. Susan gave him a look that quieted him.

"Not then anyway. My Salisbury steak was on the floor in the kitchen." He grinned, scratched his chin and then continued. "I left then, got back into my truck and headed up toward Wisconsin. I turned off I-90 at Janesville and found a campground. Well, I had a real surprise when I opened the back of the camper, and there was Lillian."

They were all listening intently. Lillian picked up the story. "I couldn't get my car started and I panicked. The camper was unlocked so I hid in there. I was terrified. I didn't really care where it was going. I was scared, too, when Bob opened the camper door, didn't know what to expect."

Bob continued. "Well, we did do a lot of talking. I fixed some hamburgers in the camper. That was our supper. Later that evening, two roughnecks came by looking for Lillian. They claimed that someone saw her leave the diner with me - which wasn't true. They were just guessing. I discouraged them from getting too nosy since Lillian was in the camper. Later she told me that she was divorced from a mob guy and that her ex and the jerk in the diner were related and would be coming after her. . . . And they did."

Liz spoke up politely and asked, "*Why* would they want to come after you?"

Lillian replied solemnly, "You can never really leave the mob, even when you're divorced. They fear what you may know and what you may say that could place them in danger with the law. The easiest solution for their problem is to make me disappear."

Susan looked at Bob and asked. "How did you get rid of them?"

"Well, the next day we headed out on I-90 through Wisconsin and into Minnesota. We decided that Lillian would be safer for the time being if she stayed with me. The two goons I had met at night were with us that day, following behind us, accosting us at rest stops, and trying to get us to stop along the road. Later, we ran into a couple of drivers who helped at a truck stop where we stayed overnight. They forcibly discouraged these two jerks from making trouble."

Ralph spoke up then. "What did these two guys want? Wanted to shoot Lillian? What?"

Lillian looked over at him and replied. "I left with something very valuable to them, although I never intended to take it. It was accidental. Also, I have a lot in my head that could be dangerous to them. They want me dead and their stuff back."

There was a hush and Bob picked up the story again.

"The next day we talked to these truckers and they stayed some distance behind us and let us know on the CB radio when the two jerks passed them. Somewhere in South Dakota they came alongside us and threatened us with a pistol, shot at us trying to get us to pull over. That's when the truckers came to our aid again. When it was over, the two jerks had rolled their car and smashed it into a wire fence. We didn't see them after that. The radio said later that there had been a one-car accident on the I-90 highway with serious injuries."

Tom scratched his head. "That's it? That's the end of it?"

Bob answered. "We didn't see anyone else coming after us. We cut through Wyoming and here in Montana with no trouble. But we are sure they will regroup and someone from the organization will be sent to find us."

"Christ, what are you going to do?"

Bob replied, "We will enjoy the company here and then move on somewhere. We need to figure this out."

"How about the law, can't they help you?" asked Karen.

Lillian responded. "Only way would be for me to go into the witness protection program and testify against them. I know what would likely happen. I've seen it myself before."

Lillian looked upset and Bob took up the conversation. "We'll think about this for a while and make some plans. There are two of us now, harder for them to get to her."

Tom sat on the edge of his desk. "Bob, I knew from what I saw that there was more to your story. Maybe we can be of help." He looked over at Ralph as if for some support.

Ralph seemed to take the cue. "Listen, there are a lot of good people here in this area that might be able to help you. We'd like it if you two would just stay here for a while, see what comes up with the goons that are after you, see what we can do about it."

Lillian spoke up quickly. "We appreciate that. But, we can't bring trouble down on you - on the people here. It wouldn't be right."

Tom smiled, "We've had our share of trouble here with Chicago goons. A few years ago…well, we dealt with it. Would you be willing to sit down with the sheriff's deputy and us and go over the details of your problems with these mob guys? I think we could come up with a plan to keep you safe, while this whole thing plays out."

Lillian looked at Bob. She reached for his hand. Tears formed in her eyes.

Bob spoke. "We don't want to be a burden or a danger to you. We couldn't bear the thought of anyone being hurt because of us …" He lost his words.

"Hey, let me worry about those things," said Tom firmly. "Ralph and I will make sure that nothing happens here on the ranch, and we'll get together with the sheriff's deputy in town and work up some plan. Then we'll see how things play out. We'll see who the mob sends out this way. Susan, Liz…what are you thinking?"

Liz looked up at her mother. Susan said, "We'd be happy to have Bob and Lillian here with us. We don't have a full booking this season, so there will always be a cabin empty. I think that we should do what we can to help them." Liz nodded energetically.

Tom stood up. "Let's all sleep on it. I'll call Allen, the deputy sheriff, tomorrow and set up a meeting for Bob in town at his office. You two can talk about what options there are."

CHAPTER 10 VIOLENCE IN ELK CREEK

Jay started the car. "Pretty good breakfast, huh?"

"Great omelet," replied Ron, then added, "Awesome waitress too."

Jay shook his head. "You better keep your mind on the job."

Ron scowled. "Okay. So where we goin'?" He stared at the map.

"I guess if we just stay on this road it'll take us to that Elk Creek town. Huh?" he asked Ron.

Ron looked up from the map. "Yeah. We go through a tiny place called Randolph first. Let's see what that's like, and then check out Elk Creek. What are we gonna say if we're stopped for something?"

"Just like we said last night. Quit worrying. We're here looking for property for our boss to invest in. We'll pick up some real estate brochures in Camden. That should work if they don't look too close."

"Here, want your coffee?" Ron held out a steaming Burger King cup.

"Set it in the cup holder."

"How we gonna find them if they're holed up at that Timberline Ranch? Can't just stroll in there. Christ, there's a six mile road into the ranch from the gate, according to this map."

"Any back roads shown on there? Gotta be another way in there where we aren't exposed."

"Don't see anything. A National Forest borders the place, but those roads aren't shown on this map. Maybe in town we can get a better map."

"We'll check this road out first. Maybe wait a while to see if one of them comes outa the ranch." Jay said. "We can't dick around too long; the word is we only got a few days to do this."

"Yeah, we'd better get it done," said Ron.

—

Tom stopped in at the Stehling cabin while Bob and the others were sitting at the breakfast table.

"Good morning, all. I just wanted to let you know that I spoke to Allen last night and he would like to see you. He said that he'd be in his office until about noon. Will you go and talk with him?"

Bob replied, "Yes. We talked about it last night. I think I'd rather Lillian didn't show herself too much in town just yet. I'll go without her."

Tom nodded, "You might want to stop in a couple of places, tell them that you're a friend of ours, and introduce yourself."

Susan asked. "You think that Bob should take our truck, leave his camper here, just in case someone is looking for it?"

"Darn," exclaimed Tom. "I'd take you but I'm hauling guests and a trailer down the road to a trailhead."

Susan looked at Ralph. He shook his head. "Maybe we could go tomorrow instead. I haven't finished changing out the water pump. It won't be done 'till late this afternoon."

"Oh, hell, I'll take my camper. It's only three miles on the road to town," said Bob.

"Maybe you should wait," offered Lillian.

Bob looked at her, touched her arm. "We don't know if there is anyone in town. I'll be okay."

Tom nodded, "You know, a good place to park your camper is behind Larry's. There's a parking spot there for delivery trucks and such. Then you can walk up to Ken's place or down to see Allen."

"The deputy has an office in the fire station," added Ralph. Ken's Diner is more toward the middle of town."

Bob gave Tom a concerned look. "Just walk in and introduce myself?"

"Sure, you bet. They'll be glad you did. This isn't Boston."

Bob grinned.

Lillian walked with Bob to his truck. She hugged him just before he opened the door. "I should be going with you." She kissed him.

"No, we talked about this. Stop worrying. I'll be okay."

"I know. I just feel guilty." She looked into his eyes.

"I love you, Lillian." He touched her face.

He opened the door and climbed into the truck.

Bob looked left and then right at the ranch gate before turning onto County Road. To the right, he saw a gray car parked off the road in the trees. He couldn't be sure at that distance, but it seemed as if there were two men in the front seat. *What the hell is that about*, he wondered? Surely, it couldn't be a cop, not on this rural spot. But it could be someone looking for Lillian. A chill went through him. He was very glad that she was back at the ranch.

He eased the truck onto the road and headed for town. A glance at the mirror showed the gray car pulling onto the road. They stayed well behind during the three miles to town. Bob turned right into the side street just as soon as he saw the fire station, and immediately turned into the alleyway behind the businesses. Then he went slowly along the alley until he saw the sign for Larry's Bar and Grill and the parking spot that Tom had mentioned. He got out of the truck and made sure it and the camper were locked.

Bob walked back to the end of the alley and looked around, but he did not see the gray car. Walking briskly to the corner, he turned and walked the short distance to the fire station and the office of the Sheriff's Deputy. Two men were sitting just inside the door, a crackle of a two-way radio interrupting the quiet. They looked up as the door opened.

"Help you?" asked the one.

"I am looking for the deputy…Allen."

"Go on out back." He gestured with his thumb. "His office is at the end of the hall." This time the other had answered. They both looked curiously at him.

"Thanks." Bob headed down the hallway.

He saw the sign next to the door. 'Deputy Sheriff, Allen Richards.' The door was open, but Bob knocked before entering.

Allen looked up, smiled, and got out of his chair.

"Hello. I'm Bob Stehling. Tom said he called you."

"Cousin to Ralph, I hear. Glad to meet you. Call me Allen. Everybody does." Bob saw a genuine smile and began to relax. He instantly liked the man.

Allen extended his hand, shook, and pointed to a chair in front of his desk.

"Have a seat. Don't have anything to offer you, usually go up to Ken's for my coffee."

Bob sat down. "Thanks, I'm fine. Say, there was a car following me from the ranch gate into town. It looked like a gray Taurus."

"Following? How do you mean?"

"I saw it parked in the trees just past the ranch gate. It looked like there were a couple guys in it. It stayed a few hundred feet behind me as I drove here. I parked behind Larry's, but I don't know where they went."

"I'll drive around when we're done here, keep an eye out for it."

"Thanks for taking the time to hear me out. I don't know what anyone can do, though."

"Well, let's see about that. Start with the short version of your story and then we'll get into details. Okay?"

"Sure. I just came to the ranch yesterday with my friend, Lillian," began Bob.

"Whoa. Start at the very beginning, please." Allen picked up a pen and started to make notes.

"Sorry. I left Lowell, Massachusetts, about a week ago. I wanted to see the country and Ralph had invited me to stay a while with him. Everything went well. I came out on I-90 through New York, Pennsylvania, Ohio, and Indiana into Illinois. When I got to Rockford, I stopped at this place for supper, called the Lawndale Diner. When I went in there I just took a seat at the counter."

"This is Rockford, Illinois?"

"Yes."

"What time of day was it?"

"Around 4 o'clock."

Allen nodded and made another notation.

"Lillian took my order and went into the kitchen. The next thing I hear is this yelling and what sounds like someone getting hit. Then I heard some dishes fall to the floor and more yelling. I thought that maybe Lillian was getting the short end of it, so I went back there to take a look."

"You went back into the kitchen?" Allen asked, eyes widening.

"Yes…I couldn't just let her get beat, or whatever was happening."

"What about the other customers?"

"A bunch of kids in the far corner with the juke box blaring, didn't act like they heard a thing. The other waitress just shook her head and said that this arguing happened all the time."

"You went back in the kitchen. Go on…." He shook his head.

"When this big guy, Vinny, I learned later was his name, went after Lillian with a mallet, I hit him on the head with a bottle. Had to hit him again when he turned on me, knocked him out."

"Still alive?"

"Yeah. I sent Lillian out of there, told her to get lost. I heard her going up the back stairs and a few minutes later came down again with a couple of bags. She tore out the back door. In the meantime, I convinced this kid, dishwasher, to get out of there and find a new job. I was outa there then and in my truck. The kids and the other waitress were still there. She wasn't happy with me, unhappy that she would have to deal with Vinny when he came to."

Allen was shaking his head and writing in his notebook.

—

Lillian looked at Susan. "How can I be useful around here? Can I help with the cabins or the lodge? I'm pretty good with mop and vacuum cleaner."

Susan smiled and shook her head. "No, no. You're our guest. Just relax, Liz and I have the routine down pretty well. There are two college girls that come in every weekday and Saturday to help us."

Liz looked up and said, "Mom, maybe Lillian could help Karen. I bet Karen would like a free hour now and then."

Susan nodded. "Maybe. I could ask her. I'll be going over there in a few minutes."

Lillian smiled. "I'd be happy to do that. I'm not a half-bad baby sitter. You have all been so nice to us. I'd like to do something."

Susan got up from the table, looked at Liz. "Better get going girl, lots to do. I'll be with Karen for a while." She turned to Lillian. "Just make yourself at home."

Lillian nodded, and glanced to the window, looking toward the road.

—

Allen looked up at Bob. "Okay, you're in your truck. You've left the diner. It's around 4:30. Is that correct?"

"Yes. I drove out of the diner and went back to I-39 and then I-90. When getting dark, I looked for a campground. I found one at Janesville, just in Wisconsin a little ways. I signed up and made my camper hook-up. But when I went to the back and opened the camper door, I freakin' near had a coronary. There she was," Bob paused.

Allen was writing rapidly, trying to catch up. "This sounds like a TV script."

"She was scared...of me...and of what had happened back at the diner. She hadn't been able to start her car and had panicked, tried my camper and found it unlocked, and hid in there."

"What'd she say?"

"She was terrified that Vinny and her Chicago mob ex-husband Joey, would come and kill her"

"Why? Why bother with her?" asked Allen.

"I guess one just doesn't leave the mob. She probably knows too much for her own good."

Allen stared at Bob. "That's it?" He shook his head. "What'd she take when she left?"

"She grabbed a bag hoping there was some money in it, but it also had an important book and CD."

Allen looked up, shaking his head. "You still have it?"

"Yes."

"You may wish you left it behind. On the other hand, it probably wouldn't make any difference if you left it or not."

Bob nodded, took a deep breath, and continued. "These two goons, they're related and report to Frank Cappella through some other guy."

"Cappella? Holy shit! Your lady friend *is* in trouble. Even out here in the sticks we heard of him. Who's the under boss that they report to?"

"Ah…I think his name is Santos. Yeah, Santos. Mike Santos," Bob replied.

"Haven't heard of him. I'll look him up on my computer. So what happened?"

"Well, that evening I was approached by two characters at the campground. They wanted to know where Lillian was, claimed that someone saw her come with me. I basically called them liars and that I didn't have any idea where she was. The one guy wanted to get pushy, probably wanted to look in the camper. I threatened to call 911 on my cell phone. That's when they went back to their car."

"Hang on." Allen tried to catch up with his notes. "What did they want?"

"They never actually said, only that they wanted to see Lillian. I was afraid that they would force her to go with them."

Allen looked up and nodded. "No doubt they wanted the bag she took."

"That and to silence her."

"Go on."

Bob continued. "Later, we decided that she should stay with me, at least until all this played out. She had wanted me to drop her off at a bus station so she could go and hide with friends somewhere, but then we realized that it might not be healthy for her friends or her. So we set out in this direction."

"You were planning on coming here."

Bob nodded. "We picked up a tail right away. They came alongside of the car and tried to force us off the road, I refused. That evening at a truck stop we enlisted the help of a couple of truckers, and when these characters showed up again, the truckers used some persuasion to make them go away."

"Like what? What'd they do?" asked Allen.

"The drivers had these tire clubs, chased the two goons away."

"Just like that?"

"Well…they had to use the clubs," Bob added.

Allen shook his head and scribbled rapidly. He looked up, "Jeez, don't stop now…you're on a roll."

Undeterred by Allen's wit, he continued. "Well, the next day, the same thing again. These two jerks came alongside and shot at us. Apparently, they lost control, for the next thing I know, these jerks are off the road and rolled it a couple times."

"Christ! Go on, what happened after that?"

"Not a thing. We made it here without any more trouble. Lillian is scared shitless, however. She is certain that this Vinny and Joey will be coming after her."

"She may be right. If she has them by the short hairs, or if they *think* she does…yeah, likely it ain't over."

"I really worry about anything happening to her. I don't want to see any trouble come to the folks at the ranch, either."

"I understand and we'll sure try to avoid that."

The phone rang and Allen reached for it. The conversation was short.

"That was the sheriff - wants to meet with me later. The new budget is due next week."

Bob stood up and extended his hand to the deputy. "Thanks. Appreciate any help at all."

"Listen Bob, you gave me plenty to think about. I want to run this by the sheriff later, see what he thinks. But you're probably right; those guys will keep looking for you and Lillian. They have lots of resources. You'll have to keep an eye on her."

"I will."

"Anyway, I'm glad you came in. I'll be getting back to you and be looking around some myself, see what strangers are about."

Allen watched Bob walk out of his office. What a hokey story. How much of this was true, he wondered? He'd have to have a serious chat with Ralph.

—

Bob stood on the sidewalk and looked around. Not much of a town, he thought; three blocks long and no traffic light. Larson's Drug Store was across the street; two cars and a pickup truck were at the curb. A storefront next to it showed a Notary Public sign in the window, but otherwise seemed a mystery. Maybe it was an accountant's office. He saw the large sign for Montana Electrical Cooperative at the far end of the street with three yellow utility trucks angled to the curb. A Preston's Lumber truck went by slowly, heavily laden with plywood and pallets of brick. There was no sign of the gray Ford that had followed him into town. Maybe he had been a little paranoid. He started walking towards Larry's Bar and Grill. He'd stop in there first, get a cold one.

He pushed open the door and entered Larry's. It looked like it had just opened. A young bartender was setting up. He looked up, smiled, and wiped down a spot on the bar in front of him. Bob sat on the stool.

"Good afternoon, just opening up. Name's Jim. Be with you in a minute." He rummaged in the sink and Bob heard the clinking of glasses and running water.

"Take your time. I'm Bob, cousin of Ralph Stehling."

Jim looked up, smiled. He reached for a towel. "Cousin of Ralph's?"

"Yep. I'm staying with him for a while. He and Tom Bauer said I should drop in and say hello."

"Glad you stopped by. What can I get you? Kitchen isn't open yet."

"Looks like you have Coors on tap. Let's do that."

"Larry said that he wanted to meet you. I'll give him a buzz."

Jim reached into the cold locker and pulled up a frozen mug. At the same time, he pushed a button that was on the wall under the bar. While he filled up the mug from the tap, the door to the kitchen opened and a medium sized man came into the bar. His tight T-shirt sleeves showed muscular arms and the tight fit revealed a barrel chest.

"Must be Bob Stehling! I'm Larry Johnson. Tom told me you were coming by. It's good to see you." With a wide grin, he reached out with his big hand and took Bob's in a firm grip.

"Nice to meet you, Larry."

"You staying around here for a while?"

"Yes. I'm staying at the ranch with Ralph and his family, me and a lady friend." Bob felt Larry's eyes quickly sizing him up.

"Hey, that works for me. You'll like being at Timberline. They are all special people. So you drove out here, huh?"

"Yeah. I have a camper on a pickup. I decided to see some of the country." Bob took a deep pull from his beer.

"Sounds nice. You'll enjoy yourself at the ranch. You plan on doing more traveling?"

Bob shrugged. "Probably. I don't have any real plans, but I'd like to see some of the National Parks."

Larry scratched his cheek. "You're right between Yellowstone and Glacier. You really ought to see them both before you leave the area."

"Yeah. I always wanted to see those places."

"Lots to see around here, too. Ralph or Tom could tell you all the neat places."

"Coming up through Bozeman and Butte was impressive. I never saw scenery like that before," said Bob.

Larry glanced at his watch. "I gotta get back to work. I don't have any help until 4 o'clock. It's been a pleasure meeting you, and please, come back. We have entertainment in the evening, Wednesday through Sunday. The food ain't bad either, if I say so myself."

They shook hands again and Larry went back to the kitchen. Bob drained his mug, dropped some bills on the counter and started to leave.

"Come back and see us," said Jim as he picked up the empty mug.

"Sure thing. Say, can I get out the back? My truck is out there."

"Sure, just down the hall. The back door is always unlocked during hours."

"Thanks, Jim. Be seeing you." Bob followed the hallway to the back door.

When Bob stepped outside, the bright sunlight temporarily blinded him. He stood still, letting his eyes adjust to the sudden change. He saw a car parked behind his camper, a gray Ford. The car doors slammed and two men moved toward him. Unease gripped him.

"What do you guys want?" he said, when the men were about eight feet away.

"Listen, Bob. It's Bob, isn't it? We want to ask you the whereabouts of our friend Lillian." The heavy set man looked in his 40's. The other, thinner and wiry, had his right hand in his jacket packet. Bob didn't like the strained, almost manic look on his face. He felt his heart racing.

"Who the hell are you?" They had his camper boxed in.

The two guys took a couple steps closer. "We want to talk to Lillian. Now why don't you get in the car and we'll go make a phone call, and you can ask her to come talk to us."

They were on him in a second. The heavier man grabbed his arm in a vise-like grip. The other poked a pistol into his ribs. "Move it old man. Get in the car."

Fueled by a sudden rage, Bob made a desperate lunge. His head slammed into Jay's face. Feeling the hold loosen on his arm, he swung around to bring his fist into the groin of the man with the gun. A bellow of rage came from both assailants. Bob swung back to smash his fist into the big man's face. The gunman swung his pistol in a glancing blow against Bob's head. Bob reeled back, stars swimming in his vision, pain searing his brain, and he fell against a couple of near-empty metal garbage cans, which went crashing against the door of the lounge. Bob tried to get up, but the two men were standing over him landing their fists into his face and torso. The garbage cans banged against the door.

The door slammed open and Larry burst out with a gun in his fist, the usual damp towel clinging to his shoulder. The bigger guy had Bob on the ground. Larry saw the pistol as the other man turned, bringing it to bear on Larry. Larry pulled the trigger. The 9-mm bullet slammed into the man's left shoulder, but he managed to hold onto his pistol in the other hand and staggered to the car. A siren could now be clearly heard. The big man lunged toward the car, as he pulled a pistol from his jacket. He got into the driver's seat, slammed the door, and the car started to move. The driver fired his pistol. The bullet missed Larry and ricocheted off the door jamb. The car roared around the camper raising a cloud of dust, and then shot forward down the alley. Larry lowered his pistol.

Bob sat up, leaning on some boxes. His face was bloody, he moaned, and his head dropped onto his chest. Larry rushed to him.

"You gonna be okay? Stay still. Ambulance is on its way."

Bob moaned, looked up at Larry through unfocused eyes. "Bastards…" he moaned.

—

Deputy Richards was about to turn off the main street to the back alley, when he saw a car sprint onto the street from the far end of the block and head away from him. Allen pressed the SUV hard, quickly coming up behind the Ford. He sounded the siren a few times. The gray Taurus roared out of town. Allen brought his SUV alongside the car, swerving into the left rear quarter. The car started to skid, the driver over-corrected, and the car spun off the highway and smashed into a utility pole. Allen stopped and quickly got out of his vehicle. The driver came out of the car brandishing a gun. When he turned and pointed it at the deputy, Allen Richards fired. The driver dropped to the ground. When ordered to get out of the car, the wounded passenger offered no resistance. Allen checked him for other weapons and then put handcuffs on him. Keeping an eye on the fallen driver, he looked quickly at the shoulder wound of his prisoner, and then sat him in the back of the SUV. A quick inspection of the vehicle didn't reveal any other weapons. Allen checked the man that he had shot. He could find no sign of life. Allen used his lapel microphone to radio for assistance. The sheriff and an ambulance would come from Camden, some six miles away. Allen trembled, felt nauseous. He had never killed anyone before.

—

Larry waited behind the lounge for the first responders from the fire station. He tried to clean the blood and dirt from Bob's face with his towel. The ambulance came up and two men jumped out. Larry recognized the EMT, and he knew Jeff well as a full time employee, at Preston's.

"Larry, what the hell happened?" Jeff leaned over Bob as Larry stood up.

"He took a pistol whipping. I'm glad you got here fast."

"Who is he? What happened?" Jeff took out his notebook, started jotting things down.

"Bob Stehling. Some goons worked him over. He's staying out with Ralph at the ranch."

The EMT had the stretcher on the ground and a backboard ready. "Jeff, gimme a hand."

"Yeah, sure." They slid the backboard under Bob, laying him flat.

Jeff turned to Larry. "Lar, did you ever see these guys before?"

"No. Looked like a Ford rental car." Larry added in exasperation, "I couldn't get the plate number."

They secured Bob to the backboard, placing the cushions and clamps on his head and torso. They worked quickly and Bob was soon in the ambulance. Jeff got into the driver's seat and they started down the alley, and onto the road to Camden.

—

Ralph came in the back door at the kitchen and smiled at Lillian. He picked up the telephone on the second ring.

"Ralph, this is Larry. We had a bit of trouble here just now."

"What happened? Accident?"

"No. Your cousin. A couple of guys jumped him out back. He came in, had a beer and we talked a little, and then he left out the back door where his truck was. Heard the racket from inside."

"Oh shit…how bad?"

Lillian went pale and went to stand by his side.

"I looked out the little window and saw these guys pounding on him. I grabbed my pistol. Jim called Allen. Then I went outside. Soon as I got out there, this one prick points a gun at me, and I let him have it. Got him in the shoulder."

"How's Bob?"

A tear ran down Lillian's face. She bit her lip.

"Jeff and the EMT guy came with the ambulance in a few minutes. By then the two assholes had gotten in their car and hauled ass up the alley. I got the one. He was bleeding all over the place. The guys took Bob over to Camden, said he'll be okay. Took a hell of a beatin'."

"Thanks, Larry. We'll head over to Camden now. Appreciate the help . . . and the call."

Lillian began to cry and held tightly to Ralph's arm.

"Say, you think you can come get Ralph's camper from out back? It's probably safe enough, but I'd feel better if you came and got it. I haven't heard from Allen, I gotta call him. He should've come by a while ago."

"Sure. Thanks again." Ralph hung up the phone and put his arm around Lillian's shoulder. He turned to her and related what he had heard. She was upset and Ralph put her into a chair. He picked up the phone and punched in the extension for the Bauer cabin. He relayed the news to Karen and Susan.

——

Allen stood by the wrecked Ford as Sheriff Wayne Crawford finished his notes. An ambulance had taken the wounded prisoner and the dead driver back to Camden. Another deputy accompanied them.

"You'll need to do the paperwork on this. Shooting creates a lot more work these days. But you did the right thing." The sheriff watched the wrecker load the smashed car onto a flatbed truck.

"Hell of a thing. I've never killed anyone before." Allen slumped against the SUV, eyes cast to the ground.

"You'll be alright. It's a tragedy, but you did the right thing. This other fellow, Bob Stehling, he's at the hospital. They had worked him over real well. You got some idea what's it's about?"

"Yeah," Allen nodded. "Bob stopped in the office earlier and told me this wild-ass story about what happened to him and his lady friend on their way out here. I got it all down on paper, but I wasn't sure I believed it. I believe him now."

"Why don't you include that statement in your report as an addendum? We'll talk about this tomorrow. Come up to my office before lunch."

"Okay. I'll be there."

"Allen, you did the right thing." Wayne went toward his vehicle. He turned as he reached his car. "Come by if you want to talk about it, or call me. Okay?"

Allen nodded and waved.

—

Tim McGuire, reporter for the Camden Gazette, was going to lunch when he heard the police scanner in his car coming alive. He arrived at County Hospital just as the second ambulance pulled into the ER loading zone. The driver, used to seeing him at accident scenes, told him what he knew of the shootings, the wounded prisoner, the car wreck, and dead driver. Tim learned that an older man named Bob Stehling had been brought in a little earlier by the Elk Creek ambulance. Here was a story, he thought, and dumped right in his lap. Forget lunch. He hurried inside to the lobby.

Jolene, the nurse at the ER station, looked up as he came through the door. She smiled as he leaned over the counter.

Did his old flame still harbor some feelings for him, he wondered?

"Stopped in just to see me? That's sweet." She smiled teasingly.

"I stopped in at Larry's the other night. Thought you might be there."

"What? On a weeknight?" She gave him a look that cautioned him.

"I hear you got a couple of customers just now. What can you tell me?"

"You know better." She looked up and frowned.

He looked at her, wrinkled his face in an inquisitive expression.

She whispered, "Some dude from Elk Creek came in all beat up. Also, a wounded guy that a deputy is watching is in the OR right now. There. Now do I get more than your smile and whiff of aftershave?"

"Jolene, you're still my heartthrob.

"Get out of here." She winked and turned away.

"What room is the assault victim in?"

"He's at X-ray, should be in 113 in twenty minutes. Only family members, until the doctor says otherwise."

Tim grinned. "Aren't I family?"

"Get out. I never talked to you."

Tim passed the time in the cafeteria with two-day old pie and lukewarm coffee. He let nearly an hour go by, and then walked down a hallway parallel to the one with room 113. At the end, he crossed over to his intended hallway, and immediately saw the handwritten tag inserted in the sign holder, *R. Stehling*. He pushed on the door, opening it a crack. Bob lay in his bed with his head well bandaged. There was no one in sight. Tim pushed open the door and entered the room.

"Mister Stehling, please forgive the intrusion. I'm Tim McGuire of the Camden Gazette and I would like your version of what happened. I won't take long. Are you up to it?"

Bob looked up; saw the young man at the door. A bit wary, he asked for the reporter's ID. Tim eagerly presented it to him and prepared to jot down notes.

"My head hurts. Don't feel like talking." Bob closed his eyes.

"I'm sorry. I'll keep it real short. Okay?"

Bob turned to look at him. "What? I got thumped on. That's it."

"Why? Who did this to you?"

"A couple of goons. They tried to convince me to go to some meeting somewhere. Mistaken identity, that's all. What else could it be?"

Tim asked a few more questions and then thanked Bob for the information, wished him well, and left the room.

Later, when Tim inquired at the Sheriff's office, he was told that the wounded man had refused to talk, had made a phone call to Chicago for a lawyer, and was still in the hospital under guard. Tim sat at his computer and looked at the digital photos he had taken. One picture clearly showed the license plate of the rented car. He picked up the phone.

CHAPTER 11 CAMDEN GAZETTE

Lillian stood next to Bob's bed in County Hospital. Tears ran down her face. He reached for her hand and held tightly. She looked in horror and sadness at his head, wrapped completely with gauze bandages, and an IV stuck in his hand.

"I'll be okay. I've got a hard head." Bob tried to make light of his injury, but the strain on his face gave away the pain.

She bent over and kissed him. "I love you Bob," she whispered.

He squeezed her hand and looked into her face. "We'll be okay."

Ralph moved up next to Lillian. "Holy cow, Bob. You aren't twenty any more."

Bob nodded, tried to grin. "Is my truck okay?"

"Yeah, we went and got it. Hey, you hear? They got those two guys. One's dead."

Bob nodded again. "Allen was by earlier, told me. Some reporter was here, too."

"Reporter? What'd you tell him?" Ralph looked a little puzzled.

"I said that it must have been a case of mistaken identity, and let it go at that. I didn't want to give him any more. Anyway, he didn't stay long."

Lillian wiped her eyes. "The nurse said that you have a concussion. This is dreadful."

"It hurts some. But, the doc said that I'd be fine in a week or so. It isn't that serious." Bob looked from Lillian to Susan to Ralph. "I'll have to be more careful," he admitted.

Susan came up to Bob, bent over and kissed his forehead. "You take care. If you need anything, just call us."

"Thanks for coming by." Bob held tightly to Lillian's hand.

She bent her head to kiss him again.

"I love you, Lillian," he murmured softly.

"I know you do."

Susan tugged on Ralph's sleeve, and they slipped quietly out of the room.

—

The Camden Gazette featured the news of Bob's assault on page 2. The article, bylined by Tim McGuire, described the assault, the shooting of one assailant behind Larry's Bar and Grill, and the pursuit of the getaway car by a sheriff's deputy that resulted in the fatal shooting of the driver when he turned on the officer with a gun in hand.

Two days later Tim prepared a follow up article, identifying the assailants. His photos of the rented car had led him to the rental agency at the Camden Airport, and from there a couple hours on the Internet and telephone got him the identity of the two assailants. The article appeared in the Camden Gazette the following day and was carried by the news wire, appearing in the Chicago Tribune a day later.

Montana Tourist Assaulted: Chicago Mob Ties Suspected
By Tim McGuire, Camden Gazette

Elk Creek, MT (AP) - Earlier this week, fifty three-year-old Bob Stehling, a Massachusetts retiree on a cross-country trip in his camper, was accosted and beaten outside a restaurant in this small western Montana town. He was hospitalized with lacerations and concussion. The restaurant owner shot one of two assailants in an attempt to assist the victim, a patron of his establishment. The driver of the getaway car, who allegedly brandished a pistol while resisting arrest, was fatally shot by a deputy sheriff. The passenger, wounded in a scuffle at the restaurant, was arrested and hospitalized in Camden. An investigation of the rented car, revealed the alleged assailants to be affiliated with known members of the Chicago mob. The retiree claims that it was a case of mistaken identity.

Joey and Vinny met at the Playpen at noon to raise a glass on Vinny's birthday, go over the past week's receipts, and hopefully to hear good news from the gunmen sent out from their Sioux Falls layover. The Playpen was among several businesses controlled by Joey and Vinny and was their favorite hangout. Mack, the bartender, had passed the Chicago Tribune to Joey when he had come in, folded to the article on page 5. Joey read it and passed it wordlessly to Vinny.

"Goddamn this bitch!" Vinny bellowed. He glanced towards the bar. "Mack, pour me another."

"I should have shut her up long ago," said Joey, his face red with rage. He whipped the newspaper across the room. "Christ, all we need now is for Frankie to hear about this."

"Christ, Joey, what're we gonna do?" Vinny tossed the tumbler of whiskey down in one gulp. "Goddamn broad could unravel everything. We *gotta* stop her!" He looked at Joey, wildness in his eye.

"Un-goddamn-believable! The old prick is indestructible. Where is Lillian? Why didn't those two morons hit *her*?" Joey looked at Vinny in anger and confusion. "You got an explanation for this?"

"They told me she's holed up on a ranch, impossible to get to. They wanted to draw her out by threatening her old-fart friend."

"Yeah, that worked real well, didn't it?" Joey's fist crashed onto the table.

Mack walked over, hesitantly, with the phone in his hand. "Got a call, Joey. Says his name is Cipriano."

Joey looked up, surprised, and reached for the phone.

"Hey, Chucko, how the hell are you? Haven't heard from you since… well, you know when."

"Joey, good to hear from you, too. I thought I'd call; see what that cluster fuck in the paper is all about. You musta seen it."

"Don't sound so damned pleased with yourself. What you know about it?" groused Joey.

"Nothin'. Just the article says it's your guys. What? Loosin' your grip?"

"What the hell you want? I'm pretty busy."

"That's why I called. Figured I could do something for you out here in Big Sky Country; get the score even between us, and do it before the big guy hears about it."

"That'd take some doin'. What you have in mind?"

"Well, maybe send a couple of *real* pros to do the job."

"Screw you, Chucko."

"I get the job done, we're even. Right?"

"You can do that, we're even," said Joey, his voice suddenly calmer. "Here, talk to Vinny, set it up with *him*." Joey handed the phone across the table.

Vinny went over the details with Cipriano of what they needed to do. He emphasized the need to recover the stolen items. Realizing it wasn't a secure phone, neither one mentioned names or particulars. Afterward, he lay the phone down, sat back, and sighed in relief.

"Joey, you think he can do it? God, I hope so."

"It'd be good for him and for us. He owes me some big ones for saving his *huevos* on that underage hank-panky bullshit he was involved in."

"Do we dare trust him?" Vinny wasn't all that sure.

"He's a giant asshole, but he wouldn't cross me. You call him tonight; make sure it's getting done." Joey's faced turned red. He slammed his glass on the table. "Damn bitch!"

Vinny, startled, ran his fingers through his hair. "Who's the guy with her?" Vinny spat the words out, his face flushed with rage and panic. "This is crazy. Who is this asshole? Sounds like goddamn superman. Shit, Joey, if *the man* hears about this…Christ, we'll be done."

"If Cappella gets a hold of it, we'll be dead."

—

Frank Cappella, boss of the Chicago crew, sat down at the kitchen table, took a bite out of his toast and picked up the newspaper. He glossed over the articles on the front page, and flipped to the next, where he read about the mayor's reelection and wondered how much that would cost him. He sipped his coffee and flipped the page, but nearly missed the small article on page 5: *Montana Tourist Assaulted: Chicago Mob Ties Suspected.*

Frank read the article, then read it again. *What the hell is this? Some of our guys? Couldn't be…better not be. Shit!* He picked up the telephone, punching in the number for his lieutenant, Mike Santos.

"Mike? Yeah, it's me.

"I'm just finishing up brunch. You eat? Wanna come over?" said Santos.

"I'm good. I'm reading today's paper…you see it yet?"

"No. Got the Trib' here on the table. What's up?"

"Take a look on page 5."

"Hang on a minute."

Seconds ticked by and then Frank heard Mike back on the phone.

"Frankie, what the hell is this?"

"You have no idea what's goin' on? These aren't your guys? What the hell?"

Frank's tone gave Mike a chill.

"Christ, Frankie…I got no damn idea."

"Okay, okay. Get out there and see what the guys are doing. Don't let on about anything. I'm goin' to do some checking on my own. We got to get a handle on this. I'll be in touch."

"Okay, Frankie. If I come across anything at all, I'll get right back to you. Holy shit."

"Don't do anything, yet. Let's not overreact. I don't want to generate any more publicity. Keep your ears open and I'll get back to you."

"Okay, Frankie."

Frank took a bite out of the toast and threw it back on the plate uneaten. His housekeeper picked up the dishes, brought him a clean cup, and filled it with coffee. Frank picked up the telephone and punched a few numbers.

"Brian, Frank here."

Brian Lorenz was Frank's accountant. But more than an accountant, he kept Frank out of trouble with the tax people and also had a knack for knowing what was going on in the organization, with the guys on the street. He had never asked Joe about his street savvy, just accepted it as a gift.

"Good to hear from you," said Brian. "I get lonely here in this fancy office you gave me."

"When you get a chance, take a look at today's paper. It's on page 5 of this morning's Trib'."

"I read it earlier. I was going to ask you about it."

"You haven't heard anything? Are these our guys? What the hell is going on? Montana?"

"I don't know anything about this. I haven't asked around, was going to talk to you first."

"I want to keep a lid on this. Something like this could blow up in our face, and we can't control what happens then."

"You're right. I should look into this."

"Listen. Be careful. Don't create a lot of dust. But find out who these renegades are. If they're in my organization, I want to know right away, and what the hell it's all about."

"I can get started right away."

"Great. I really appreciate it. I want you to look into every business that we have going, every goddamn one of them. Costs, expenses, intake, outlay, everything. I'll see if there's something here I'm missing. If you get any trouble, get hold of Santos or me. Brian, this is crazy. What the fuck am I missing?"

"I'll get right on it. You can reach me on my cell."

"Okay." Frank hung up the phone. Had he lost touch with what was going on in his own organization? Was this just the tip of the iceberg? He reread the news article.

CHAPTER 12 OLD HOMESTEAD

Two days in the hospital seemed like a lifetime to Lillian. Bob was finally coming home. Ralph turned into the hospital and found an empty spot in the 30-minute loading zone, where he parked the truck.

"Ralph, we girls can sit in the jump seat. Let Bob sit up front, more room," volunteered Susan.

"Sure, I'm sure he'd appreciate it." He turned to Lillian and winked, "I'm betting he'll be glad to see *you*."

"I guess I hadn't realized how much I loved that guy until lately," replied Lillian.

Susan nodded. "He's kinda crazy about you, too."

"Even with all this…all this trouble. I feel real peaceful being with him," she replied.

Ralph looked at Lillian. "I remember Bob as conservative and kinda quiet. I never would have dreamed that he would just pull up stakes and take to the road. Amazing."

"He's gutsy," said Susan.

"Yes, he is." Lillian looked sadly at Susan and Ralph. "I'm sorry that I'm bringing all this trouble to you."

"Oh, for Heaven's sake, stop saying that already. We're glad you're here. You and Bob are special." Susan took Lillian's arm and they entered the hospital.

An orderly wheeled Bob out of the hospital and helped him get seated in the truck. A short time later they were on their way home.

"I am so glad to be out of there. They're nice people, but I just want to be back with you folks. I really do appreciate the time and trouble that I put you through, taking you away from all that you have to do."

"Oh, shut up. It's been no trouble. Everything at the ranch gets done. We have wranglers and a couple of hands; not to worry." Ralph grinned at Bob. "You're full of surprises."

"Lillian's going to have to keep a better eye on Bob, can't let him out by himself," said Susan, grinning.

"I'm sticking to him like glue from now on," said Lillian as she squeezed Bob's shoulder.

Ralph looked over at Bob. "They jumped you behind Larry's, huh?"

"They were waiting for me, parked behind my camper. I'd seen that car earlier, in the trees across from the ranch gate."

"What'd they say they wanted?" asked Ralph.

"They wanted me to get in their car, take me to a phone where I should call Lillian so they could talk to her. They poked a gun in my ribs."

"Damn. Then what," asked Ralph.

"I got angry. I managed to land a couple of good ones before they hit me over the head with the gun. When I went down they started to work me over with their fists. That's when Larry came out the back door. I guess one of the guys pointed a pistol at Larry. Not a good move on their part 'cause that's when Larry shot him. I'm not real clear on it. An ambulance came. I guess someone called it."

"Oh Bob…" sobbed Lillian.

"Allen came by the hospital and told me the rest of the story."

"Yeah, Allen had to shoot one of them. The guy died," said Ralph.

"I'm sorry…sorry that Allen got in that spot," said Bob softly.

"I talked to him," replied Ralph.

Lillian wiped her eyes and said, "We should leave."

Susan rejoined, "I told you already, I don't want to hear that talk. We're okay with it. So's Tom. So quit it. You're both going to relax and get Bob healed up."

"You heard her," said Ralph, looking over at Bob.

Bob hesitated as he reached for the bread. "Would it be okay if we hiked away from the ranch? I really need something to do and to get some exercise."

Susan looked up from her lunch salad and frowned.

"I'm trying to talk him out of it," said Lillian.

Ralph scratched his chin and slumped back in his chair. "You know what Tom said the other day, remember?"

Bob nodded. "I remember, sure. I don't mean to be unappreciative; it's just that I need to do something. I just can't sit here." Bob looked down at his plate and toyed with his food.

Ralph scowled. "The only thing keeping those goons at bay is the six miles of road out to the gate. They could storm this place, but it would take a lot of them. Right now the bad guys are worried about getting away if they get caught on this road. So I imagine they're keeping an eye on this place with binoculars and waiting for their chance. If there are only a couple of them, they'll try to catch you well away from these buildings or out on County Road." He paused. "You go walking into the hills or out into the meadows, you're taking a big risk."

"How about up the old logging road? That go anywhere?" asked Bob.

"A few years ago we had trouble here with some criminals that came in through the National Forest and then onto the logging road and down here to the ranch. It was a hair-raising experience. These guys might figure it out as well." Ralph looked at Susan. She nodded.

"What happened?" asked Lillian. "Someone get hurt…a robbery?"

"We'll tell you about it later," said Susan. "It's just that it isn't safe for you to wander around too far."

"If bad guys are around, they'll be trying to figure out how to get to you. They could be on foot or in a Jeep. Hell, they could be on a horse," added Ralph.

Bob nodded. "Okay, okay."

"I've got to get going. There are a few guests that want me to show them some horsemanship. It'll keep me busy for a couple of hours." Ralph got up from the table, took a last sip of his coffee, and was out the door.

"Let's watch Ralph and the guests at the corral," suggested Lillian taking Bob's arm.

"Liz should be out there somewhere," said Susan. "She'll be working with Sioux."

Bob forced a smile. "Okay."

A couple of days later, Bob's restlessness overcame the caution that his friends suggested.

"We're thinking of hiking out along that overgrown track of a road, the one that goes east through the meadows," said Lillian to Susan at breakfast.

"It goes on forever, nearly six miles to the end. It's unprotected. Someone with binoculars could spot you and head you off." Susan didn't look up, but picked at her food.

Ralph took a sip of coffee. "I talked to Tom last night. He suggested that if you just *had* to do something, that it would be safer if you took that old red hay truck from behind the barn, and drove it out along the meadows to the abandoned Holbrook homestead at the east end. That way if anything suspicious occurred, you could high tail it back."

"They could take a radio with them. The new models have enough range, don't they?" Susan looked up at Ralph.

"Yeah, the new ones should work out to ten miles. There's a spare hanging in the barn by the rack with the chaps and slickers."

Bob looked at Lillian. "Want to do that, take the old truck?"

"Sounds like fun. Appreciate you guys letting us do that," said Bob.

Susan looked at Bob. "There is still risk. Please be attentive and come back quickly if you see anyone."

"We will. Thanks, again."

"Please stay to the old track; that way we know where to look for you if you don't come back by dark." Susan looked at Bob and Lillian and shook her head. "Take water with you. Grab a roll of toilet paper, too. I'll fix you some lunch."

They set out just after 10 o'clock on a cool morning with a clear sky.

"I don't think Susan is too thrilled with us being gone," said Lillian as they bounced along the dusty track in the well worn truck.

"No, I don't guess she is. Ralph either," Bob replied. Crossing a dry creek bed, Bob shifted the transmission to a lower gear. That was met with a groaning noise from under the floorboard.

"That doesn't sound good."

Bob shifted again, and it quieted. "This baby has got a lot of rough miles on it. Odometer doesn't work anymore."

The mountains rose steeply to their left as the ranch disappeared behind them. Meadows, green with spring growth, seemed to spread endlessly to their right and ahead.

"All's quiet out this way. I don't see any of the cattle."

"I don't see anything moving out there at all." Lillian put binoculars to her eyes.

"Where'd you get those?"

"Hanging on the wall with the radio." She pulled the radio from her pocket. "Do you know how to work this?"

Bob took the radio and toyed with the controls, then handed it back to her. "It's pretty simple. Let's keep it turned off, save the battery."

Lillian pointed out the old buildings, just becoming visible above the grass. "There's the old place. It sure is overgrown."

Bob stopped the truck in front of the cabin. "Let's just sit a minute, make sure no one else is here."

"This is a really cute place. There's a little corral and a barn," said Lillian.

"The barn needs some help; part of the door is off. The cabin looks good from here, though."

"Susan said the cabin's been shuttered for almost ten years."

Bob peered out the windows, but didn't see anything moving. "Let's get out and take a look. I think we're alone." He yanked on the door handle, but had to put his shoulder to the door before it opened. Lillian came around to his side and wrapped her arms around his waist, pressing her head against his chest.

"I don't ever want to lose you," Bob said softly.

"You won't. I kinda like you." She looked up into his eyes, smiling.

He kissed her, and she wrapped her arms around him.

"I love you," she said.

Heat surged upward from the swelling in his loins. He pulled her against him, his hand moving down her back. She moaned when his hand found her thigh. Gasping, she playfully pushed him away.

"You're well, no doubt about it," she said, a wry smile playing on her face.

"Maybe later?" he asked.

"Later is better."

She took several steps toward the cabin, and then turned when he didn't follow her. Bob was looking out into the expanse of the meadow. She walked back.

"What is it?"

Bob pointed to something in the distance.

"What do you see?" She strained to see what Bob had noticed.

"A couple of riders, maybe 200 yards away, headed toward the ranch gate."

"I see them. They seem to be going straight ahead, though. They probably didn't see us in this tall grass," said Lillian, shading her eyes. "Should I get the binoculars?"

Bob stared as the riders moved off to the right, seemingly in the direction of the gate. "No. It's got to be a couple of wranglers. Ralph mentioned yesterday that they had to move a bunch and put them in a different pasture."

"I wonder…" She didn't finish her thought.

"Let's just stand still until they're out of sight," said Bob. "They haven't seen us."

She put her arm around his waist. He felt a shudder go through her. He held her against him.

Before them stood the abandoned log cabin, and past it a small barn with one of the doors fallen off. Next to it was a small corral and an old well with stonework and collapsed wooden roof. These were the remnants of the Holbrook homestead. The place spoke to them of times past, of families and lives come and gone. They both felt sadness as they talked about it.

"Want to eat lunch before we look inside?"

"Sure," said Lillian "This is a lovely picture, just sitting right here."

"Like a postcard."

Bob pulled out a tarpaulin from the truck bed and spread it on the ground. Lillian took out their lunch from a canvas tote sack.

Bob dropped to the ground next to Lillian.

"Let's eat."

Bob was looking toward the cabin and barn as Lillian placed a napkin in his lap.

"It's beautiful, isn't it?" she said.

"Uh-huh."

Lillian passed him a sandwich. "I hope we're not upsetting Susan and Ralph."

"They don't want anything bad happening to us. They would feel guilty if we got hurt. I understand their concern. It's just that I have a hard time just sitting around. Maybe it's selfish on my part."

Lillian looked at Bob. "If you want me to, I'll go to the FBI."

He reached for her and pulled her gently against him. "Would things be any better? You'd still have to watch your back."

"It's just so much trouble for you and for the ranch. I feel guilty."

"I could talk to Allen about this, see what he thinks. But then, I would have to tell him everything. The sheriff might insist on bringing the FBI into it. They would want the stuff you have. Things would get complicated."

"What should I do?" she asked.

"I'm hoping that they quit coming after you. That it becomes less important to them. Wishful thinking, I imagine."

"Maybe under normal circumstances, my taking the stuff wouldn't have produced such a response. But these two guys were stealing from their boss, and the proof of it is on the CD and in the book." Lillian paused, shook her head slowly. "I think they'll keep coming after me until their boss gets wise to them. I'm surprised that they got away with it for so long, several years."

Bob stood up for a moment and looked into the distance. There were no riders or any movement but for the swaying of the tall grass. The time passed quickly as they talked about their childhood and school years. The hours alone allowed them to explore each others hiding places, where fear and haunting memories stood in the shadows. It was a strangeness that both tiptoed in, where fear and uncertainty was assuaged by a gentle touch or a caressing look.

They wondered what life here would be like, away from all that had been comfortable to them in the past, away from those they knew. The values here seemed different, with a reliance on one's abilities and one's close friends. This seemed to be a place where friendship was the glue that held it all together. Friends had been important in their life before, but this was different. It was at the core of who these people were.

He kissed her, and she snuggled close. His roving hands were now eliciting moans. She suddenly stood up, her face red. "Not here...not like this," she gasped, then bent over and kissed him. "God, you're an animal."

"I think you were right. I'm all better." He grinned teasingly and got on his feet.

"I'll say."

Bob picked up the lunch papers and bags and stuffed them into the tote bag.

"Let's look at the old buildings." Lillian tugged at his sleeve.

Bob removed a piece of baling wire that had been thrust through the clasp and then pushed against the heavy wooden door of the cabin. Rusty hinges and an accumulation of dirt resisted movement until Bob threw his shoulder against it. He peered inside but couldn't see much because of the shutters which were closed on the two windows.

"Can you open the shutters on this side?" asked Bob. "It's dark as a tomb in here."

"Sure." Soon light came in through the window into a room that appeared to be a living area. A wooden table and chairs were situated directly under the window. An old beat up sofa was at the far end of the room against an adjoining wall. There were also a rocker and an easy chair with stuffing hanging out of it.

"I think the mice have been busy here," said Lillian pointing to the chair and sofa.

"Mice, yes, but I don't see signs of anything bigger."

"There is a kitchen off to the right," said Lillian. She peered into the dim light. "There's a stove, a sink and a hand pump, even a potbelly stove. No one's been here in a long time."

Bob nodded, "I have to agree. Is that a bedroom back there?"

Lillian poked his ribs teasingly. "Don't get any ideas. We've got to head back."

Bob grinned. "I'll take a quick look." He went to a doorway of a room made into the far corner of the cabin. "There's another window in here, but it's shuttered, too," said Bob.

Lillian looked over his shoulder. "I bet the mice had a nice time on that bed."

"Yeah, the stuffing is all over the floor."

"You know, this was probably a really cute little place when folks lived here. I bet this place could tell a story," Lillian mused.

"We'll ask Ralph about it."

They stepped back outside and Lillian closed the shutters again. Bob was examining the exterior construction when Lillian came up to him.

"These logs are still in good shape. The chinking is falling out but otherwise it isn't bad. The foundation stones look good; nothing moved over the years."

Lillian put her arm around Bob's waist. "I kinda wish that we lived here. Silly, maybe, but I really like this spot."

Bob pulled her to him, kissed her, and said, "I'd like that too - with you."

She tugged at his hand. "Let's look at the barn, *then* we'll go."

"Okay. It'll have to be fast. We need to head back."

They walked over the half of the barn door that had fallen off the hinges, and peered into the gloom. Light filtered in from the loft windows, and they heard several birds chirping in the rafters.

"It's probably a regular zoo in here," commented Lillian Bob took a few steps into the barn, interested at looking at the construction. Some boards had fallen from the sides of the barn and light poured onto the floor from those openings. Piles of hay and rusted farm implements lay about on the floor. The stone foundation seemed intact, although the sideboards looked in poor condition. Surprised, Bob didn't see any daylight coming through the ancient roof. As they walked farther into the barn they could hear the scurrying of small animals, and the flutter of wings as sparrows lifted to the eaves.

"The floor is just hard packed earth, but the drainage around the barn must be good. I don't see any damage to the foundation. It looks tight."

"The sideboards look like they're a good wind from coming off," commented Lillian.

"The sun probably did a job on them. But look, the roof is intact. Now, that is amazing for such an old place."

Lillian looked up at the roof. "Seems like there is a hay loft at the other end."

"We better get out of here, need to get back." Bob tugged her sleeve.

"What a neat place," Lillian mused as they left the barn.

—

Frank Cappella picked up the telephone on his desk.

"Yes, Maria?"

"I have Mister Santos on the line, can you talk to him?" she asked.

"Sure, put him through. I'll use code-08 this time."

After a moment Frank heard the secure connection click in. "Hey Mike, what've you got for me?"

"I've been nosing around some, dropping in at the Playpen and at our package store on Treadwell Street."

"Yeah, what are you hearing?"

"I don't have anything definite yet. But when I show up, everybody goes mute. Its okay if I want to talk about baseball or whatever, but when I ask about business and finances, they know nothin', want me to ask the bookkeeper. I left three messages for the goddamn bookkeeper, haven't heard back. I get the feeling that someone is scurrying around covering their ass."

"I've got Lorenz out stirring the pot. He'll be looking into all the books. Keep this to yourself. But, if Brian runs into any foot dragging he'll ask you to help him out. Okay?"

"Yeah, sure. Something ain't right, I feel it."

"We better get a grip on this soon, before a shitstorm rains down on us."

"Okay."

"Be talking to you." Frank hung up. Anger and fear stirred his thoughts. He picked up the phone again.

"Maria, find Lorenz and ask him to give me a call."

"I'll track him down," she said.

She was a gem, he thought. Lucky to have her walk in for a job. And, just outa prep school. He'd have to give her more challenging work to do. He didn't want to lose her.

—

Susan looked up from the cooking stove and smiled as Lillian and Bob came through the back door. "Liz convinced us to hold supper for you two."

"Thank you. It was such a nice day. Time just went by so fast," replied Lillian.

"Did you see anyone out there?" asked Susan.

"Saw a couple of riders when we first got there. They were far out in the meadow, headed in the direction of the gate."

"That must have been the wranglers. There was a bunch of calves to be brought in for their shots."

"It sure is a beautiful place. The old cabin and barn, we looked all through it," replied Bob.

"That's the old Holbrook homestead. That place is long abandoned, need to ask Ralph." Susan looked at Bob and then Lillian. "Liz picked up a phone call while Ralph and I were over with Karen. Wait, here she comes now."

Liz pulled off her boots at the kitchen door and entered. She smiled at seeing Lillian and Bob. "How was your day? Picked up a phone call for you."

"Who?" asked Lillian.

"He wouldn't say. He wanted to talk to you, wanted me go find you. What a jerk. When I asked if there was a message, he said no, that you'd know what it was about." Liz shrugged her shoulders.

Bob frowned. "Could you tell where he was calling from?"

She shook her head. "I was out in the laundry room. The phone there doesn't have a display. Was it them?"

Bob nodded, "No doubt."

Liz refilled the coffee cups and picked up the supper dishes. Bob and Lillian finished describing their day and the beauty that had impressed them so much at the old homestead.

Ralph took a sip. "The old Holbrook place has been abandoned for quite some time. The old folks died about ten years ago. The heirs live back east somewhere and they've been fighting for years over the inheritance. I don't think they know what to do with the old ranch. They were city folk. So it just sits there. Tom asked about buying it a few months ago, but never got a reply from their agent."

Lillian asked, "They still own it, don't they?"

"I guess so. There's been no one out there, and now there's a tax lien on the place. The state is ready to declare it abandoned property."

"It sure is a lovely place," added Lillian.

"Ralph, do you think Bob and I could drive out there and take sleeping bags and some food? We'd love to stay there overnight, get a real feel for the place."

A scowl crossed Ralph's face. "Listen, guys. That phone call tells me that someone is around here again and looking to find you. It won't be a social call when they do. I don't feel right about you two wandering off for a day . . . not even for a couple of hours."

"Me neither," said Susan without looking up.

Ralph looked at Bob. "There's an overgrown track of a road that runs out to County, and it's only two miles long. It's a lot easier for those guys to get to you when you're up there."

"Would they even think to look there? It's nowhere near the ranch, at least in their minds."

Ralph shrugged. "You are probably right, but who knows what they're thinking."

Ralph glanced at Susan. "If you got your mind set on it, I have a couple extra sleeping bags.

Lillian beamed and grabbed Bob's arm. "Oh, that would be great. We'd really appreciate it."

Ralph's voice turned serious again as he looked at Bob. "What are you going to do about those clowns that are chasing you? I think the only reason they haven't come right up to the door is the long road into here. If anything went wrong, they might not get away."

Bob nodded. "I thought of that."

"They're killers, after all. I've asked the wranglers to keep a good eye out and call on the radio if they see anything suspicious."

Bob glanced at Lillian. "If I may borrow your old truck again, I'm going to see Allen tomorrow. I think it might be time to have a serious talk. I'm sure he'll want to know more than what we've said so far."

Ralph shook his head. "Be careful when you leave here. Don't go out that gate if you see anything suspicious. We don't want to have to visit you in the hospital again." Ralph looked at Bob and grimaced.

Bob relaxed when he didn't see a car near the ranch gate. He pulled the old hay truck onto County Road and turned toward Elk Creek. It was a warm, late spring day, and he rolled the window down to enjoy it. Once he reached town, he turned into a parking space in front of the firehouse. He didn't see any traffic on the street. Bob pushed through the door, nodded to two men sitting by the window, and walked to the back of the building. Bob tapped on the door frame of Deputy Allen Richards's office.

"Hey, Bob," Allen grinned. "Stayin' outa trouble?"

"So far. You get to talk to the sheriff about all this?"

"Hell, yes. I had reports to fill out, meetings to go to, and we sat for a while and went over what happened and what you told me. Of course, that piece in the paper - people are asking questions down at the courthouse. Sheriff has some questions for you, too."

Bob cleared his throat. "Sorry. Say, you know Liz?"

Allen nodded.

"She picked up a call for Lillian while we were out in the meadow. He wouldn't leave a name or a message. This is spooking us some. I was wondering if you had any thoughts about it."

"Do you know where the call came from?" asked Allen.

"No, there's no caller I.D."

"I wonder if we have another set of goons in our midst."

"Lillian and I are rather nervous about coming into town or going to Camden."

"Yeah, I bet."

"I need to tell you more of what happened. Can it be off the record?" Bob shuffled his feet.

"I don't think I can do that. I'm obligated…" Allen was shaking his head, twirling a pencil between his fingers. "Maybe you need to talk to a lawyer first."

Bob nodded. "I better ask Ralph about one."

"Wayne did say he was sure there was more to what was happening than you let on."

Bob scratched his head, smoothed his hair. "Yeah…"

"Anyhow, we're doing some more checking between Camden and here."

"Much obliged."

"We'll be checking at the airport, see who's renting a car, things like that. We'll be parking close to the ranch gate at times, see if there's any strange traffic. We'll try to get a handle on this."

"I think Susan and Ralph are getting a little spooked, too."

Allen looked up. "I gotta tell you, these guys aren't novices. Be on your toes. You can see a long ways down your road from the ranch, so if any strange car comes up, call immediately. Don't wait." He handed Bob a business card. "After hours, the phone rings at my house on the fifth ring. If something happens, you call."

"Okay. I appreciate anything you can do." Bob shook his head. "I'll probably see a lawyer. I don't know how this will end."

"Stay in touch."

"Thanks. I'll walk down to Larry's, say hello. I sure appreciate the help the other day, saved my ass."

Allen grinned and chuckled. "You didn't do too bad, yourself."

CHAPTER 13 WOLF MEADOWS

They bumped along in Ralph's old truck, planning to stay overnight at the abandoned ranch site.

Ralph turned to Lillian. "You know, the old Holbrook place could probably be picked up for a song. It's abandoned."

Lillian looked up at him, but then Bob asked, "How much you think?"

"Well, probably pick it up for back taxes."

"How many acres?" asked Lillian.

"Several hundred, I'd guess. And, there is the easement to County Road. It would make a nice little place, big enough to have a horse or two."

Bob thought out loud. "Of course, there's a lot more cost involved in getting the place to be habitable. You got to update the cabin, grade the old easement; then there is the well, don't know what kind of shape it's in. You'll want to put in an electric pump. You won't want to use a Port-o-potty, so the septic system will have to be looked at. There's no electricity or phone, that'd be several thousand to get the lines run in."

"Cell phone doesn't work at all out here?" asked Lillian.

Bob shook his head. "Doesn't work south of Elk Creek. I checked that the other week."

"I imagine the electric company will charge quite a bit to run in lines."

"Uh-huh. And Tom says we'll need a generator for emergency use. Power goes out every now and then."

"Are they expensive?"

"Nothing compared to what the electric and phone will cost," replied Bob. "We'll have to dip into the wallet for 15-20 grand to fix it all up. And, who knows what the back taxes are."

Lillian glanced up at Bob. He winked at her. The old cabin and barn came into view and Ralph stopped the truck. They got out and stood looking at the scene.

"It is so still and lovely," she said as she hugged him.

"Let's get this stuff over to the cabin. We'll open it up, air it out, and chase out any critters living in there."

Lillian hesitated, looking at Bob. "You think there may be any snakes?"

"Ralph said there weren't any bad ones around here. We probably have some mice and chipmunks that won't be too happy with us moving in."

"Okay."

"I saw a couple of old brooms in there, I'll sweep it out and then we can see what we got."

—

Maria opened the door to Frank Cappella's office and let Brian Lorenz and Mike Santos enter.

"Anything else, Mr. Cappella?" asked Maria.

"Hold all my calls."

She nodded and closed the door.

The three men took seats at the conference table. Lorenz reached for the coffee and poured one, Santos declined. Frank already had a cup sitting in front of him. He looked at the two men and saw the nervousness in their faces. He would try to keep a grip on his anger.

He looked at Santos. "Somebody better start talking."

Mike cleared his throat. "We've been at several of our places, still a few more to go. Need to go out to Rockford, too. Anyway, I went to our clubs here in town, starting at the Playpen. Seems like the bartenders are playing it pretty straight. I met a few of the waitresses afterward, bought them breakfast, and they all seem to think the bartenders are okay. Also, the bartenders are reporting they've seen state tax people there, generally once a week. I guess they use the same guys over and over and they know them now." Mike paused and looked at Frank.

He nodded, "Go on." His face didn't give anything away. He was slowly stirring his coffee.

Mike squirmed in his chair. "These tax guys being there every week, something is up. I looked at the stock, checked the inventory, nothing jumped out at me. Someone gave the alarm though. The next place I went into, Ponytail, they were expecting me. The place looked like it had been spit-shined. Stopped at a couple of the package stores. They also knew I was coming. The books *looked* clean, at least when I checked the stock. Funny though, I didn't see either Joey or Vinny at any of the places. I asked where they were; everyone gave some lame excuse. *Oh, he was just here; Yeah, you just missed him.* This is all pretty odd. I didn't press the issue, because you said to keep it low key."

"You never saw Joey? Vinny either?" asked Frank. The stirring stopped momentarily.

"No. Some of the girls said that they've been in every couple of days, so they *are* making the rounds…when I'm not there."

"Brian, talk to me," said Frank. He took a sip from his coffee and set the cup down.

Brian stopped wringing his hands. "I went into the places that Mike did, but a day or two later. I focused on the books, cash register receipts, and liquor inventories. Then I compared all this with what Joey and Vinny had given me earlier for tax purposes, as well as their month-closing reports."

Frank was looking intently at Brian now. He started to stir his coffee again. "Are these state guys on to something?" he asked.

"I think so. I don't have it all analyzed, yet. But, it looks to me that at every place I was in, there is reason to suspect that money is being skimmed. Like Mike said, I think the bartenders are fairly honest, and the state isn't likely to see anything there. What I think I see is a difference between what is delivered by the bottling companies and the amount of liquor being sold, maybe a 30 percent difference." Brian paused, glanced at Frank, and then continued. "I went to the bottling companies and checked our receipts. They look legit. I have to do a more thorough analysis, now that I have copies of all the records. The big problem will be the state tax people. They'll eventually get wind of this, and then there'll be hell to pay for all of us. If they find any discrepancies, even at the bar, they can subpoena all the books.

Frank poured more coffee into his cup and slowly stirred in a splash of cream. They were silent around the table. He slammed the spoon on the table, staring at one, then the other of his lieutenants.

"I don't have to tell you how serious this could be. If the state guys get into our records, then the feds will be here the next day. We'd be looking at some serious time in the joint." Frank paused, his eyes boring into them. "I don't even want to think of what the Family will do if we bring this shitstorm down on them."

"What should we do, boss?" Santos brushed the sweat from his brow.

Frank glared at Santos. "Find out where Joey and Vinny have been for the past year, who they saw, who they screwed, all of it. Work with Brian and find out about the money going in and out of their personal accounts; where it went, where it came from, how much."

Santos nodded.

Frank, tapping his finger on the table, turned his attention to Lorenz. "Work up a report on the finances of every place we have. A separate report for each place. No copies. Nothing on the computer. Bring it to me personally." He looked over at Santos. "That goes for you, too. No computer and no e-mail."

They sat silent; they hadn't been dismissed. Lorenz was wringing his hands slowly. Frank looked from one to the other and his face darkened.

"Most guys who get put away get caught for tax evasion. This amateurish bullshit could be our undoing. Focus on this. I want to hear from you every day in person here in this room, not on the phone. I have this place swept for bugs every few days and I have these special windows. Okay, gentlemen? Remember, no phones, no computers."

Frank stood up. Lorenz and Santos pushed back their chairs, picked up their notebooks and shook hands silently with Frank. When the office door closed again, Frank took out a package of Rolaids, put four in his mouth. His stomach hurt.

He trusted Lorenz and Santos. There wasn't any person smarter than Lorenz, he thought. He knew how to get to the bottom of things. He had the street smarts, too. Santos had been a good soldier some years ago, a silent and efficient enforcer on the street. Maybe he was out of his element, trying to manage all the business interests. They had to get through this crisis, and then he'd reorganize.

—

The open windows allowed a steady breeze to flow through the cabin, dissipating the musty odors. Lillian finished up with the broom while Bob took all the bedding outside to air it out and dislodge any critters still at home.

"If we lay these two mattresses next to each other on the floor, we can put our sleeping bags on them. There's enough stuffing left to be useful. Better than the bunk beds, huh?" She gave him a wry grin.

He smiled, raised his eyebrows momentarily, "*Much* better." Looking at her as she moved with the broom, he felt a warmth flow through him. It seemed that he had recovered 15 years of his life during the last month. He couldn't recall when he last felt so alive.

They walked through the few cleared acres around the cabin and barn, where nature was trying to reclaim it with aspen saplings. Their conversation was about what would be needed to make the place habitable if they were to buy it. Bob jotted ideas in his little notebook as they took a close look at the cabin and barn. They were amazed that both roofs were still serviceable. The barn needed a new door, and the residual hay and junk would have to be removed to form a clean and dry floor. Bob could smell the rotting wood and hay, and expected that there would be a zoo underneath it all. The old place had no electricity and he worried it would be expensive to bring it in from County Road. Lillian went to the well that stood between the cabin and barn, and vigorously pumped the cast iron handle to no avail. Bob brought the water bottle and poured in enough to get the pump primed. Then he took up pumping. They were both surprised to see water pour from the spout after a minute. He jotted a note that the water would have to be tested, and an electric pump sunk into the well.

When they came to the old track that was the easement to County Road, they realized that a grader would have to redo the surface. Brush and chest high saplings had taken over since the old folks had died, and the road was all but obscured. Bob stared down the old track but couldn't see anything moving. He scanned the horizon toward County Road, but there was only the swaying grass and fluttering aspen. *Hell of a place for someone to hide. I wonder who's out there.* Bob put his arm around Lillian's waist.

"I'd like to live here with you," said Lillian.

"I'd like that, too."

As they walked back to the cabin, Bob turned to her. "We need to ask ourselves if the serenity and solitude here is what we both want."

Lillian looked at him and nodded. "Uh-huh, we do need to be sure. Let's sleep on it."

"We should."

She hugged him. "I'm glad I'm here with you."

They passed a thermos of coffee between them. They had long since devoured all the food Susan had packed for them. The night was cool, and they wrapped themselves in blankets.

"The moon is coming up." Lillian pointed to the eastern ridge a few miles away.

A light fog was settling into the meadows, close to the ground. Some distance away, a cow was bawling.

"We should have almost a full moon tonight. I guess some of the cows are up this way, hadn't seen them earlier."

Lillian replied, "The grass here is so high, we probably just didn't see them. The growing season isn't very long, is it?"

"No, the first frost comes in mid September, sometimes earlier, according to Ralph. He told me that they turn out the cow-calf pairs in the beginning of May and by early October the calves have gained almost 600 pounds. Can you believe it?"

"Amazing. Ralph said that this was all good grass," added Lillian.

"I'm sure they fatten the calves in feed lots before they go to slaughter."

"I still hear them," said Lillian. "Must be a lost calf out there somewhere."

"I hope that the momma calls it in. A calf by itself away from the group is an invitation to the wolves."

"It might be injured."

"Shhh, listen."

"Wh…what?"

Then she heard it, too, a howl in the distance. She grabbed Bob's arm, pressing herself against him. In a few seconds they heard other howls.

"They're here tonight, coming into the meadow," said Bob.

They heard intermittent barks and howls, and they were getting closer. "Don't have to worry about the bad guys if the wolves are around," said Bob. "They're coming through the meadow, must have come up through Tom's place."

"It's scary," she said. Then added, "But a beautiful sound."

"Beautiful, unless you're an injured calf."

They heard the cow continue to bawl, others seemed to have joined in. The barks and howls were in front of them now, far in the meadow, coming from the same direction as the cow's alarmed bawling.

Lillian asked, "Will they attack us?"

"Not likely. They're probably looking for an injured calf that got separated."

"I feel sorry for the calf, but I have to admire the wolf. It's such a wild and intelligent creature. I read in the paper that the wolf issue was pretty controversial."

"There's a lot been written about their social structure and how they impact the environment."

"I don't guess that the ranchers are too keen on it though," commented Lillian.

"You're right. Many secretly kill them when they get a chance. Occasionally a wolf will pull down a calf, especially if it's sick or injured. I don't think Tom's lost any calves to them, but if he did, I'm sure he'd have shot the wolf.

"Oh listen, they're off to the left now, they're moving."

The barking and howls came in a chorus as the pack moved eastward through the meadows.

"Wolves have a large area to hunt in, and might not be back the same way for a week," Bob offered.

"Wolf Meadows."

"Huh?"

"We can call this place 'Wolf Meadows.'

He looked at her and smiled, turned her head up and kissed her.

———

Mike Santos sat down in the large corner booth at the Lawndale Diner. He opened his briefcase, and pulled out the folder with his notes. He turned to a clean page. A young waitress appeared with water and a menu. Mike looked up at her and smiled when she asked what he wished. *Probably her first job,* he thought to himself.

"Coffee, please. Would you grab me a Danish?"

"You like that heated?" she asked.

"No, thanks. Please ask Vinny to come out here, need to talk to him."

She looked at him curiously. "Sure. I'll get him," and then turned toward the kitchen.

She soon returned with the Danish and coffee. "He'll be right out."

"Thanks."

Mike took a sip from his coffee and bit into the Danish. He heard footsteps, looked up to see Vinny coming from the kitchen, wiping his hands on a towel he then tossed onto his shoulder.

"Mike. Hey, good to see you." He extended his hand. "Ginny taking care of ya?"

Mike wasn't smiling. "How ya doin', Vinny. It's been a little difficult getting to meet with you and Joey. Know where he hangs out?" Before Vinny could respond he continued. "Sit down here for a few minutes. Like to go over some things." He put the briefcase on the floor and Vinny sat down.

Vinny ran his fingers across his beard stubble. "You know, I haven't seen Joey in a couple of days. A bead of sweat glistened on Vinny's brow. "Dunno. He's usually at the Playpen unless he's making his rounds."

"It's damn near noon, where are all the customers?" Mike looked around. "This place used to do well."

"It's been slow." Vinny shrugged and glanced at the few notes that Mike had made. "The new Denny's down the street ain't helping."

"Vinny, you know it is *essential* that we make this a going proposition to complement the business in the back." Mike looked directly at Vinny, a challenge in his eyes. "You *know* that."

"Yeah. I had a few problems. I hired this new waitress, still looking for a dish washer," he mumbled.

"I'm hearin' that you were disrespectful to the help, even got physical. That's why she and the dishwasher left. That's what *I'm* hearin'."

Vinny kept his eyes lowered. "We had disagreements. It got outa hand."

"How 'bout you go print out the financials for the last couple of months. I want to see how we're doing here. We'll talk about it."

"I…things got a little crazy." Vinny's face was ashen. "Lillian, she…took my backup CD and my record book."

There was a hard edge to Mike's voice. "What? What are you talking about?"

Vinny kept his eyes lowered. Sweat ran down the side of his face. "We got into this argument. When she left,…she…she took the stuff and some money. Crazy broad…"

Mike slapped his pen down on the table. "You got no backup? Is that what you're telling me?"

Vinny sat back as if slapped. There was no mistaking the threat in Mike's voice and in his icy stare.

"I hadn't done it in a while."

Mike raised his voice. "You fool! She took your record book, too? What was in it?"

Vinny wiped the sweat from his face with his fingers. "It had my accounts, the names, the numbers, payments…stuff like that."

Mike cracked his knuckles and sighed. "Where is she now? Have you tried to contact her?"

Vinny squirmed in his seat. "She's gone. Left here with some guy. Last I heard they were in Montana. I sent some guys to find her…get back the stuff…make sure she doesn't talk."

Mike's hand slammed down on the table. "And what happened? You screw that up too?"

Vinny jumped. "They haven't been able to contact her. This guy she's with…"

"And who gave you permission to do that?"

"Joey…we…I…"

"Shut up!" Mike's face had turned red. He stood up, opened his briefcase, threw in his notes and pen, and slammed it shut. "You stupid shit! You're staying here. Don't leave until you hear from me."

Vinny nodded.

"Stay close to the phone. *Don't* make me come look for you." Mike picked up the briefcase and walked to the door.

Vinny watched as Mike drove away. He felt sick, and went to a shelf for a bottle of Maalox, opened it and tipped it to his lips. What would happen if it all came to light? He went to the phone and punched in Joey's number. There was no answer.

—

Light poured in through the open windows. Sunrise was only minutes away. She had abandoned her own sleeping bag during the night. Lillian pressed her body closer to Bob, their legs entwined, their bodies soaked in perspiration.

"God," she gasped. "You are such an animal."

Bob's chest heaved. "Can't get enough of you."

She ran her lips over his face. "I'm glad."

"It's cold," she said, burrowing her face into his neck.

"I bet you wish you had some hot coffee."

"Oh, would you?" She showered his face with kisses. "Please?"

He untangled himself and got out of the sleeping bag, letting in the chilly air.

"Oh, I'm freezing," she whimpered.

"Stay in there. It'll take me a while to get a fire started. I don't think anyone will see it in the daytime." He started to pull on his clothes.

"You sure?"

"Give me a half hour or so. Close your eyes."

She smiled, and pulled the sleeping bag over her head.

Lillian came out of the cabin with a rolled-up sleeping bag under each arm. She put them next to the other items that would go back to the ranch with them.

"I feel kind of grubby," she wrinkled her nose.

"We can take a hot shower back at the ranch. Here, want some coffee?"

She sat down next to him. "I'm getting to like you."

"Here, some coffee will fix that," he grinned.

She leaned into him and kissed him, then took the cup. "I like it here. Sure, it's a lonely place, but we don't have to be alone when we don't want to be. There are people at the ranch all the time, and then Camden isn't far away. This place gives me some real peace."

"I didn't know that I would like it so much either. It's certainly growing on me. Elk Creek is a neat little town despite all the crap we've been through. There isn't much here, but it feels right. Yeah, I could be talked into staying here."

—

"Yeah, we got here fine." Nick had the cell phone at his ear while Leon opened the minibar in the motel room. Nick had called Chuck Cipriano as soon as they had arrived in Camden.

"I gotta ask. How bad you want these guys? I know you said you wanted to get the stuff they had, but there is nothing but space out here. Looking at the map, that ranch is six fuckin' miles off the road. They'd see us comin' long before we got there. There might be a back way, but it'll take time to check it all out."

Chuck spoke in measured tones. "Don't have time. Get it done. Do it right. No cops. Do it and get the hell out."

"It's a guest ranch. If we charge in there we'll likely be getting in with 15-20 people. If you want the stuff, it could get messy. There'd be fallout," cautioned Nick.

Chuck paused.

"Boss?"

"Yeah. Here's what ya do. Give it a couple days. Figure a way to get one of them when they leave the ranch. Probably the guy with the camper. The broad will probably stay back. Grab the guy and get him to talk the woman off the ranch for some reason. Figure out something."

"Like what?"

"He's got to come off that ranch sometime. When he does, grab him. If you tell him you're gonna chop off a couple of fingers, he'll call her."

"Okay, but that could take a while, maybe a week. We have to figure out some cover for being in the area. You got to see this place. I mean, there is nothing out here."

"Just get it done, next few days."

"Got it." Nick slipped the phone into his shirt pocket and took the small bottle of Jim Beam that Leon handed him.

—

It was after ten o'clock when they got back to the ranch. They met Ralph as they walked toward the lodge with their sleeping bags.

"How are you two this morning?" he asked, with a wry grin.

"Great," said Lillian smiling.

"It is a nice spot. Maybe you two ought to stay around here, huh?" He winked. "Or have you already decided to do that?"

"We were talking about it. We both like the place. You say it's available, huh?"

"Yeah, abandoned, at least by the owners of record. You could make a nice little spread out there. You guys really thinking about this?" Ralph looked at them.

Lillian and Bob both nodded. "Would you and Tom be okay with it?" Bob asked.

"We'd love having you here. I'm just hoping it's what you two *really* want to do. It'll sure be different from what you're used to."

Lillian looked at Ralph and nodded. "It feels right, though."

—

Frank Cappella came into the outer office. "Good morning, Maria."

She looked up and smiled. "Good morning, Mr. Cappella. Mr. Lorenz called. They're both at the Sheraton in Rockford. Newspapers and coffee are on your table."

"Get him on the phone. Scramble on code-01 today. No interruptions until I finish." He went into his office. *I've got to give her a bonus soon.*

He poured a cup of coffee, sat at the conference table, and spread out the Chicago Gazette. He scanned each page, reading the articles on the upcoming mayoral election, looking for any surprise news items from Montana. His telephone rang.

"Mr. Cappella, I have both your parties on the line," said Maria.

"Go ahead and put them through."

"It's Lorenz. I'm here with Santos."

"What've you turned up?"

"Mike visited the diner while I went into the truck operation next door. They were expecting us, and tried to make everything look efficient and aboveboard. I'll let Mike tell you."

"You guys see Vinny?" asked Frank.

"Mike here. I caught up with him at the diner. When I asked about the broad and the dishwasher kid, he blows me off, says that they walked out one day on some dispute. Then I asked him to print out the month's financials, and the bastard says the broad left with the CD with the files and his record book. I was ready to kill him."

Mike paused but Frank didn't speak. "It was near noon and place was empty. I told Vinny that I was coming back and that he had better be ready, and that I wanted the whole story. I had the kid's address and social security info in my laptop for withholding tax, so we paid him a visit."

"You went to his house?" Frank sounded alarmed.

"Yeah. He lives with his parents, across town. We coaxed him to tell us about what went on at the diner. It's just fuckin' amazing!"

Frank's voice had an edge. "What do you mean, amazing? What the hell is going on?"

"The kid tells us that this stranger came in about a month ago. Some old guy who just wanted some supper. Anyhow, about then Lillian and Vinny get into it and he starts hitting her. The kid says this has happened before. Anyway, the stranger hears the noise and yelling and goes into the kitchen, and when Vinny picks up a mallet and goes for Lillian, the stranger whacks him over the head with a bottle. When Vinny tries to get up, this guy whacks him again. While Vinny is lying there, this old guy tells Lillian to get out of there, to leave the place. Well, hell, she lives upstairs. So she runs up and comes down a couple minutes later with a couple of bags and disappears out the back door. Meanwhile, this old guy is telling the kid that he, too, should get out of there, and not come back. So the kid left."

"Holy shit. Is Vinny crazy or what?"

"He ain't saying much to us. He's a surly bastard. From the looks of things, business at the diner is way the hell down since that little episode," said Mike. "He doesn't keep any files on his computer; only on the CD the broad took. What bullshit. Anyway, we can't see what the financials are. They gotta be lousy though."

"Joey show up there?" asked Frank.

"No. Vinny says he hasn't seen him."

"What's happening in the back?"

"They're running a pretty steady flow of trucks. The operations are going okay. There hasn't been anyone snooping around according to Sal, the manager there."

"I know Sal. You and Brian got a look at the books?" asked Frank.

"Yeah, but I don't think they tell the real story. We called some of the drivers on these logs, just random selections, and each one of them gave us an inventory number different than what is on the books. It looks like Vinny and Joey are raking almost twenty percent from the take, before we see it, and then we give them their share besides. When we asked Sal about it, he said he didn't know anything about it"

"Goddamn those two bastards!"

Brian added, "It isn't just the skim; if the state or fed tax people find out about this, its tax evasion. It looks like everything that Joey and Vinny are involved with is being skimmed, and we are going to be hung out to dry, since it is *us* that sign off on the taxes. If it comes to it, those assholes will get a free ride for turning on us."

"Did Vinny send someone after Lillian?" asked Frank.

"Yeah. Vinny sent some guys to get back the CD and the record book and to close her mouth."

"What guys went after Lillian? I want to know."

"Okay, Frank."

There was silence for several seconds, and then Frank spoke. "I want a definitive report."

"Mike and I should spend another day at it, and get some more from drivers. Another day or two and I think we can wrap it up here."

"These drivers, don't tell them too much."

"They think we're making an audit, that's all."

"Okay. Take care of it and get back here."

"Couple of days," said Brian. He heard the click. Frank had hung up.

Ralph and Tom listened as Bob and Lillian expressed their desire to make a home at the abandoned ranch site. Ralph and Tom were skeptical, and expressed concern that the isolation of the place would become a problem. They didn't want their friends to go into this venture without considering that life here would be very different. It was almost midnight when they ended the discussion.

Tom leaned back in his chair and smiled. "Well, if we can't talk you out of it, we'll sure be happy to have you both as neighbors. Of course, Ralph and I will be here to help out when you need a hand. It won't be easy or cheap to get that place running."

Ralph looked at Lillian. "I'm worried about the jerks that called here looking for you. We can't just ignore it. They could get to you anywhere, as soon as you step off this ranch. And out at that old place, you'd be sitting ducks. How is this going to end?"

Lillian dropped her gaze. Bob said, "There is no easy answer. The guys who are sending these goons out here are crazy and desperate. If Lillian talks, it would go very bad for them. I'm hoping that Allen or the sheriff could make one of these guys talk. So far, that hasn't happened. I guess we'll just play it by ear, hope for the best."

Tom shook his head. "Why not just put everything in the hands of the law?" Tom asked.

Bob spoke hesitantly. "I stopped in to see Allen a few days ago. But I couldn't talk to him off the record."

"Well, if you go to town take the old truck. Leave yours here. It might help."

Bob nodded. "Thanks."

CHAPTER 14 TROUBLE

Bob looked about nervously after he stopped the truck to open the ranch gate. Tom suggested that he visit his own attorney, in order to start procurement of the abandoned property. Tom was sure that he could also advise him on the questions that he had about the criminals, and that Bob should be forthcoming, that all would be confidential. Lillian had wanted to go with him, anxious to be off the ranch for a day, but he had persuaded her to stay behind, that the risk for her was still too great. He looked around as he closed the gate again, but didn't see anything alarming. He accelerated onto County Road.

He drove slowly through Elk Creek. A few miles farther and he came into the somewhat larger town of Randolph. It looked like a larger copy of Elk Creek, except he noticed many bars, one in each side of the street in every block. *This must be a wild place on Saturday night.* The town had two traffic lights. He turned right at the second and found a parking place near a new office building. Sam Lorimer was on the third floor. Bob entered the well-appointed office and announced himself to the receptionist, who ushered him into the lawyer's office.

They briefly introduced themselves, and in a few minutes they were discussing the purchase of the abandoned property. After a brief phone call, Sam announced that the County had a tax lien on the place for the amount of $8,530. Sam agreed to discuss with the County what exactly was necessary in order to purchase the property. In the meantime he would hire Steve Connell, surveyor, to draw up a current property plan. Bob gave him a check for the retainer. They talked for a few minutes about restoring the old place, before delving into Bob's other concerns.

Later, walking to the truck, he thought over the past hour. *Well, I've got to start somewhere.*

Bob pulled off the road onto the ranch road in front of the ranch gate. He waited for the dust cloud swirling around him to settle before opening the door. He heard two car doors close and glancing in the mirror saw two men walking toward him. A blue Taurus was parked behind him, he was boxed in. *Goddamn it, I'm getting tired of this shit. Who are these assholes?* Heat surged up his collar. His heart rate increased, he felt a sense of foreboding. *Aw, shit,* and he stepped out of the truck. He started toward the gate to unlatch it.

"Hey there. It's Bob isn't it?" asked the heavier of the two.

"Who wants to know?"

"Don't scare him to death, Leon, he's just an old fart," said Nick, grinning from ear to ear.

Bob stood still, keeping his back against the front fender of his truck. "Who the hell are you?"

"Bob, we're gonna take a little ride, back towards Camden. Cell phone doesn't work out here, and we need you to make a call to your lady friend. Have her meet us in town with what she stole from her employer."

When Bob didn't respond, Nick raised his voice. There was an edge to it. "Hey, Bob! You followin' me so far? Should I talk slower?"

The smirk on the punk's face angered Bob. He wanted to smash his fist into his disrespectful mouth. But, he told himself that he couldn't let his temper get the best of him. He had to think. What was he going to do?

"Who are you guys? Who sent you out here?" asked Bob, trying to keep calm.

"Come on old-timer," said Leon, "Get in the truck. Nick here will drive." He turned toward his accomplice. "Get his keys, let's get goin'."

Nick came forward. "The keys, Pop. Gimme the keys." He held out his hand.

"I'm not going anywhere with you two. Who the hell sent you?" Bob felt heat under his collar.

"The keys, asshole; gimme the damn keys," exclaimed Nick. He reached toward Bob, starting to feel his pockets for the keys. Bob suddenly drove his knee up into Nick's groin and sidestepped against the truck.

"Old fart, my ass," said Bob.

Nick cried out, his hands went to his groin, bending over in a spasm of pain. Leon moved toward Bob, pulling a pistol from the small of his back. In a flash, he was against Bob, ramming the pistol under his chin.

"You old fart, that was a big mistake. Get your ass in the fuckin' car, now. Open the back door and get in." He pushed Bob toward the car. Nick was still yelling and swearing in pain.

Bob looked at the car, only a couple of paces away, and knew that if he got into it, it would all be over. He couldn't let that happen. He started walking toward County Road, some fifty feet in front of the gate.

"Hey, shithead! Where the hell you goin'? Don't make me fuckin' shoot you." He stepped toward Bob, who kept walking away.

At the pavement edge, Bob faked a stumble, dropped onto one knee, and picked up a stone in his fist. Lenny was on him almost immediately, and Bob felt the gun jam brutally against his neck.

"Alright you feisty old goat, get the hell up," yelled Leon. "Get up!"

Bob felt the pressure of the gun muzzle against his neck. He could feel Leon against him, and realized that he was bent over him. Then, mustering all his strength, Bob propelled himself upward while he swung his fist around toward Leon's head. Leon tried to duck but lost his balance and Bob landed the rock hard against his temple. He heard the loud crack of the pistol. But Leon was on his knees. The gun lay in the dust.

Bob saw Nick, out of the corner of his eye, moving toward him, and he dove for the gun. He grabbed it, and as he rolled to face Nick, a few feet away, he pulled the trigger. Nick stopped, looked down at his leg, his pants now smeared with blood, and then dropped onto his knees with a cry of anguish.

Leon roared up onto his feet, blood running down the side of his head. He went to Nick, balled up in pain, reached down behind him and pulled the gun from under Nick's belt. He swung the gun upward, roaring in rage. Bob pulled the trigger again. The bullet tugged at Leon's sleeve. Leon fired and missed. Again, Bob pulled the trigger. This time the bullet ripped into Leon's shoulder. His gun dropped to the ground. He gripped his shoulder, roaring in pain and rage and started forward. Bob brought the gun up level to his eye and aimed at Leon's head.

But they heard a siren approaching. Leon froze. A glance at the road and Bob saw a sheriff's vehicle sliding to a stop. Allen quickly approached, gun in hand.

"Stay where you are. Nobody move!"

Allen went up alongside Bob, reaching for the gun in Bob's hand. "I got it, Bob. Let me have it."

Bob let go of the gun as Allen pulled it from him. Allen was quick to pick up the other gun lying in the dirt. He put handcuffs on Bob's two assailants, amid protests and cries of pain. He quickly recited their rights, and turned back to Bob. He grabbed him by the arm and brought him toward his vehicle, where he called the sheriff's office in Camden and asked for assistance and an ambulance.

"Stay here. I'm going to see what I can do for these two." Allen opened the door. "Sit down and *stay here.*"

Bob nodded. His hands were trembling. He felt a chill. He looked at the two criminals, moaning in agony. He hadn't *wanted* to shoot anyone. It all had happened so fast. Fear crept up his spine; he was in serious trouble now, he thought. He watched Allen work to stop the bleeding from the wounds. He was glad he had insisted Lillian not come with him. Initially he had felt a bit guilty, but not now.

Allen stood up, cleaning the blood from his hands with a squirt bottle of disinfectant. He looked again at the two prisoners and walked over to Bob.

"You okay?"

"Yeah. Damn glad you came along. Thanks," said Bob Allen saw the trembling in Bob's hands and ashen appearance. From the back of the vehicle he brought a blanket and wrapped it around him.

"Just sit still. You're a bit shaken. We'll have the medics take a look at you."

Bob only nodded.

"I saw these two in Camden earlier, but I wasn't in my vehicle at the time. I started after them as soon as I could. I wanted to follow them, but they gave me the slip before I could catch up. I thought that I'd better head down this way; that these two were probably up to no good."

"Really glad you did. I was running out of tricks."

"You're freakin' unbelievable. Every time I see you, you're in some kind of trouble." Allen grinned and shook his head. "The sheriff had me triple the patrols between Camden and here. We've been keeping an eye on things."

"I don't even know how it all happened, just a blur."

"There's going to be an investigation, but don't worry about it right now."

Bob turned to Allen. "We're planning to stay here. Lawyer's working on it."

"You're staying here? Oh shit, we'll have to put on a couple extra deputies." Allen was grinning.

A short blast from a siren alerted them to the approach of the sheriff, the Elk Creek ambulance was right behind him. Wayne Crawford and a deputy got out of the car. Wayne nodded to Bob and turned to Allen.

"What have we got here?"

"A couple of gunshot wounds."

Wayne waved the EMTs to the two prisoners. "What the hell happened?"

"According to Bob, when he pulled up to the gate he was boxed in by these two. They wanted to kidnap him to get him to give up the woman, Lillian. I guess he wasn't going to go easy. Got his hands on one of their guns." Allen nodded toward Bob. "I'll get the whole thing down on paper later. Bob is a bit shaken."

"Okay. Have the EMTs take a look at Bob before they leave. I'm calling in the DA." Wayne went back to his vehicle, and Allen walked to the prisoners, by then with new bandages and compresses on their wounds. The prisoners were then put on gurneys and taken into the ambulance, strapped in with restraints. The deputy that had come with Wayne got into the back of the ambulance. Before leaving, one of the EMTs examined Bob.

Allen came over and watched. "Bob is a tough old guy, ain't he?"

The EMT chuckled. "He'll be okay. His heart rate and pressure are back down."

The ambulance pulled away. Wayne looked at Allen. "You'll have to do the paperwork before you go home. I'll go back to Camden, have these two booked on assault and battery for now. I'll check with the DA and maybe file attempted kidnap in the morning. I'm sending a detective down to your office. He'll get the story from Bob and see if we need to hold him. You take Bob to your office. Get the report done so I can have it for the DA in the morning, and when the detective gets there, sit in on the meeting."

Allen nodded and looked at Bob. "Okay?"

"I'll need to call Ralph and Lillian."

"We can do that from the office."

"Oh crap," exclaimed Wayne as a SUV drove up with a stringer from the *Camden Gazette.*

"If it ain't Tim-freakin'-McGuire," said the sheriff sarcastically. Tim walked briskly toward them, camera in hand, tape recorder hanging around his neck. "Didn't take you long to get here. What? Slow news day?"

"I was having a sandwich, heard you on the radio and came right here." He reached for the tape recorder switch.

"Whatever," said the sheriff as Tim began the interview and took digital pictures of everything and everyone. The sheriff explained that two men had been taken to the hospital with gunshot wounds, but that the incident was still under investigation and a statement would be issued in Camden later.

Bob sat in the back of Allen's SUV, watching nervously as the sheriff talked to the reporter. He recognized McGuire from his brief interview in the hospital. Now, he realized, the news of Lillian and his location would be all over the newspapers. He had to talk to Lillian and Ralph, had to make sure they understood what had happened. He wondered if he would be arrested and charged with assault or even attempted murder. A shiver went through him.

Bob heard the sheriff tell McGuire he could not interview anyone, that a statement would be available around six that evening. The sheriff nodded to Bob as he walked back to his vehicle. McGuire went back to his car.

Allen turned to Bob. "Okay, ready to go to my office?"

Bob nodded.

Bob called Lillian and Ralph as soon as he was in the deputy's office. Lillian started to cry and had handed the phone to Ralph. Bob gave Ralph a short version of the story and handed the phone to Allen. "He wants to talk to you."

"Ralph, can you come by around 9:30? We should be done here by then," said Allen.

"He'll be okay," said Allen in response to Ralph's question. "Might have to testify in court. Don't know yet."

"Fine. See you then," Allen responded.

Bob looked down at his hands, as he twisted his fingers together. "What's going to happen now?"

"The detective will be here in a few minutes. Tell him exactly what happened. No opinions, just facts. He'll come at you several ways, so stick to the facts."

Bob spent all evening with Allen and the detective from the sheriff's office. Allen tried to make Bob comfortable, getting him coffee and sandwiches, while the detective bored into Bob's story from a variety of directions. It was after nine when the detective completed the interview and Bob signed his statement. He was cautioned not to leave the area, that the investigation was not complete, and that his testimony might be required. Ralph arrived to take Bob back to the ranch.

It took Bob quite a while to calm Lillian when he returned. Later, they lay on the bed, holding each other.

"I get so crazy when you leave me here and go in town. I get sick with worrying about you."

He kissed her wet cheek. "I'm sorry. I didn't want those creeps to get near you."

She said softly, "I'm going with you next time. You won't talk me out of it."

"Okay. How 'bout going as husband and wife?"

She sat up abruptly in astonishment. "What?"

He smiled. "Will you marry me?"

Tears started running down her cheek again. She reached her hand to his face, her fingers caressing his cheek. She looked at him speechless.

"Will you?"

She came into his arms. "Yes. Yes. Oh, Bob."

He held her as she sobbed and then showered him with kisses. "I love you so much."

"I love you too."

It was a glum mood at breakfast the next day. Liz prepared the food while everyone took a place at the table. No one had gotten much sleep. Tom and Karen had come over that evening wanting to know the details of the assault. There had been a lot of head shaking and worried looks. Lillian and Bob agreed not to announce their engagement, yet. They'd wait for a more cheerful occasion. They all looked up when the kitchen door opened. Tom walked in with the newspaper.

"Good morning. Just came back from town and picked up the morning paper. Bob, you made the front page." He handed the newspaper to Bob, pulled out a chair, and smiled at Liz as she handed him a cup of coffee.

Bob read the article aloud. It described the assault by two assailants, whom the sheriff later said had come from Billings, but who had otherwise declined to provide any information, beyond the name of their lawyer. The sheriff had stated the two men were in the NCIC database, which alleged they were mob affiliated and been previously arrested for truck hijacking and armed robbery. The article questioned a possible link between this event and the previous assault on Bob in Elk Creek.

Tom looked at Bob. "There's no hiding from anyone anymore."

Lillian looked down at her hands.

"They didn't leave me much choice," Bob mused.

Ralph turned to Bob and Lillian. "Hey, listen. Tom and I were talking last night and we think, in light of the circumstances, that it would be better if the land title for that property be written in my name. When all this clears up, then we "sell" it to you. That way no one sees your name show up on the records and doesn't raise any red flags with the DA or whomever."

"Yeah, it'll be a month or two before all this stuff gets ironed out with the DA and courts," added Tom. "This way, we've got the property locked up and we just transfer it to you later."

Lillian looked at Bob, her eyes tearing up.

"This is really most generous of you both," said Bob. "We don't know how to thank you."

Tom stood up. "Damn, just stay out of trouble." He grinned, pushed his chair in. "Gotta go. Guests arriving."

CHAPTER 15 THE NOOSE TIGHTENS

Cappella walked into the office at the rear of the Playpen, a *Chicago Tribune* under his arm. Santos and Lorenz were seated at the large round table. Their summons had been terse and explicit. Cappella took off his coat, and waited to sit until the cocktail waitress arranged the coffee tray and departed. Then he tossed the paper onto the table.

"Page four, read it!" he ordered his face reddening. He sat down and reached for the coffee.

Santos opened the paper to the article while Lorenz looked over his shoulder. Cappella picked up a doughnut from the tray, took a bite, and reached for his coffee. He listened as Santos read it aloud.

Montana Tourist Assaulted Again: Sheriff Sees Chicago Mob Ties Elk Creek, MT (AP) Fifty three-year-old retiree, Bob Stehling, previously on a cross-country trip in a camper and staying with relatives in Elk Creek, was allegedly accosted a second time and beaten on a rural road. Deputy Sheriff Allen Richards, on routine patrol, put an end to the altercation. The two alleged assailants were arrested and transported to a local hospital with gunshot wounds. Stehling was transported to the sheriff's office for interrogation but, to date, no charges have been filed. The two alleged assailants were carrying identification listing addresses in Billings, and reportedly had previous arrests and links to organized crime. According to Camden sheriff Wayne Crawford, the investigation is ongoing. Additional charges may be filed.

When Santos put the paper down, Cappella's eyes were boring in on him. "What the hell is this?"

Lorenz sat back in his seat. Santos looked apprehensive. Cappella put down his coffee cup and looked hard at his lieutenants. "This thing is going to stop right now."

Santos felt his stomach cramp. He forced the trembling in his legs to stop. "Frank, I haven't been able to get to Joey. No one seems to know where he hides out. The girls out there," he pointed to the door into the club, "They say that he's in and out almost every night. Sure as hell not when I'm around."

Lorenz looked at Cappella. "You have the report we prepared. Joey and Vinny are cleaning our cupboards. It's 100 percent certain. I don't know where they stash all the money, probably some account in the islands. Vinny is pleading stupidity, claims he doesn't know what Joey is doing. However, Vinny and Joey are joined at the hip."

Santos picked up the conversation. "Frank. This," he banged on the newspaper, "has got to be Vinny's doing, trying to cover his ass, since Lillian took his records. If he had names and addresses and accounts in the book, this is real serious."

Cappella looked at Santos. "Get me the phone. Bring it here."

As Santos hurried to the corner desk, Cappella looked at Lorenz. "I heard from *my* boss this morning. Didn't call to wish me a nice day." Cappella scowled. "We're stopping this right now."

Lorenz nodded his agreement.

"You'll make sure that all the books are clean, that there are no other records for anyone to find, that the tax guys can't make a case on us. You will *make sure* of this."

Brian nodded. "It'll be done right."

"Mike, I am going to fly into Camden myself, see what's happening there, and straighten this out. I've met Joey's ex-wife, Lillian, on several occasions. I've heard the rumors over the years about the FBI. She's a stand-up broad. I think this trouble is Joey's doing. She's just running scared from him and Vinny."

Santos looked up. "I always thought she was a lady."

Cappella stared at Santos "I'll be taking an ExecuAir charter. They'll get a car for me. I intend to be back home by that midnight. When I return," he paused and looked directly at Santos. "I fully expect that these out-of-control guys will no longer be a problem for us. Clear?"

Santos nodded.

Bob and Lillian were completing the cleaning and varnishing of the wide plank floors in the old cabin. They had abandoned the idea of sanding them. They decided instead to keep the old patina, and some of the history of the old cabin.

Bob and Lillian had come back to the Stehling's home well before dark. Susan had asked them to join her and Ralph at Larry's Bar and Grill with the Bauer's for a Saturday evening out. The ranch guests, as usual, had departed by early afternoon. Now cleaned up from the day's work at the old cabin, and dressed in their good clothes, Bob and Lillian went to the Stehling's cabin. When they entered the kitchen, Susan pulled a paper from under a thumbtack on the wall by the phone and handed it to Lillian.

Susan looked anxiously at Lillian. "This call came earlier this afternoon. It was not like the others. This man was very polite, and he really wanted you to call him. He said that he wanted to put an end to your trouble and his. I said I would be sure to give you the message."

Lillian looked at the note, read and reread the name, *Frank*. The color drained from her face.

Bob asked, "Who is it?"

"Frank. Frank Cappella."

"Who is *he*?" asked Susan.

Lillian looked at Bob and then at Susan. "He's Joey's boss's boss." The note trembled in her hand.

"What's going on?" asked Bob. "Do you think it would be wise to talk to him, or just more trouble?"

Lillian stood quietly for a few seconds, and then turned to Bob. "Maybe this is a good thing. Maybe Joey and Vinny have been found out. The boss, a capo, doesn't normally bother with underlings. He gets someone else to deal with them. Maybe I *should* call him."

"Aren't you afraid?" asked Susan. "He knows where you are."

"Yes, but, I think he's just finding out about what those two have been doing." She paused, "I'm sure that if *Cappella* had wanted me dead, I wouldn't be standing here."

"If he laid his cards on the table, it would be good. Maybe he did catch onto those guys. Why else would *he* call?" Bob said.

Susan looked at Lillian with concern. "We can talk about it with the boys when we get to Larry's, see what they think."

Lillian nodded. "Okay. We better get going before Ralph and Tom come looking for us."

They had pushed several tables together when Larry appeared from the kitchen with his trademark wide grin and damp towel over his shoulder.

"It's sure good to see you all here together." He then turned toward Bob. "Well, I see they haven't got you down yet. You have more lives than a cat."

Lillian put her arm around Bob's shoulder and pressed her head against him. "He's very special," she said.

"Larry, have you met Lillian?" asked Tom.

"No, but I am delighted." He shook her hand. "You've got a feisty one here," pointing to Bob.

"He's a handful."

"Well, here's Ronnie. She'll take good care of you." One of the evening waitresses came up to the table as Larry turned to go back to the kitchen.

Tom introduced Bob and Lillian to his favorite waitress. She took their order for drinks.

"Lillian, Bob…why don't you tell us about the phone call," asked Susan.

After they recounted their earlier discussion, Karen asked, "This Frank Cappella, do you trust him enough to sit down with him?" She sounded incredulous.

"These guys are killers, mob goons, aren't they?" Tom asked.

"Frank Cappella is a capo, the boss of the crew that my ex-husband, Joey, belongs to. Frank doesn't do the dirty work, although he certainly could. He normally gives that to his enforcers."

Susan asked, "Didn't the people that came after you work for this same boss?"

Tom added, "He would have had to know, somehow blessed it."

Bob spoke up then, "We're thinking that her ex-husband and the goon that worked for him, this Vinny guy, were skimming from the businesses run by that crew. Lillian had some hints of this when she was there. If that's so, no one knew about it, certainly not Cappella."

"Hard to believe," said Tom, shaking his head.

Lillian continued. "When I left there - the diner that Vinny ran - I took his CD files and a book with all the accounts information. Not a good idea, I know, but I was ripping mad and not thinking straight. Vinny and Joey must have sent those guys after us. They'd be lower level guys, not pros, lucky for us."

Bob added, "If somehow this Cappella guy found out what his guys have been doing to him, or if he read articles about Chicago mob activities out here, I imagine that he will be feeling some heat about now. This may be why he wants to talk to Lillian, to make this problem go away."

"Sounds crazy," said Tom, again shaking his head.

"Could be true, I guess," said Ralph thoughtfully.

Tom looked from Bob to Lillian. "If you think this is a good idea, we should make sure that you are safe doing it. If he comes here, it's got to be in a public place. Make him come here to Elk Creek. Try for Friday evening, few people around, he won't get too nervous. Have him come to Ken's Diner by himself. I'll talk to Ken. Since he's usually closed in the evening, it'll work out good."

Bob frowned, "Yeah, but will Ken go along with it?"

"Leave that to me," Tom said. "Look, Ralph and I will be in the kitchen. I'll ask Allen to park a couple of doors away and stay in his car. Bob, you'll drive Lillian to the diner and drop her off. Then you'll park beyond there a few doors away and stay in the truck. Lillian will take her stuff and walk into the diner, meet with this Cappella guy, and leave. Bob, when she's back in the truck, head home. Ralph and I will wait until Cappella leaves, then we'll lock up and leave, too."

Bob was nodding. "Sounds like it oughta work."

Ralph was in agreement. "Yeah, he wouldn't dare do anything; he'd know he was being watched, and there's plenty of daylight left at 7 o'clock, this time of year. You can read a newspaper outside until 9."

Lillian looked at them calmly. "I've thought a lot about this, and I don't think there'll be any trouble. I think he's got trouble already. I can't imagine that the Chicago family would tolerate this kind of attention in the press. No, I think Cappella is probably wanting to put an end to something he lost control of, and to do it soon."

"I believe Lillian is right about this," said Bob. "The last thing that this capo guy would want is *more* trouble."

Karen looked at Lillian. "I believe her, makes sense to me. We could make sure it goes well, couldn't we?" She looked at Tom.

Tom nodded, "Sure. Ralph and I will be there. You tell us when, but try for Friday night. I'll talk to Allen and Ken tomorrow." Then shaking his head again, he smiled at Bob and Lillian. "It sure is exciting being around you two."

Lillian looked first at Bob, then at Karen and Susan. "When this trouble is over, Bob and I are getting married."

Bob grinned from ear to ear. Tom's jaw dropped open. Ralph just stared.

Susan stood up, went to Lillian and hugged her. "Oh, this is wonderful!"

"When did all this happen?" asked Karen, smiling broadly.

"Bob popped the question last evening." Lillian put her hand in his.

"Congratulations. I really mean that," offered Tom.

Ralph scratched his chin. "Bob, I can't keep up with you. But, I'm really happy for you both."

Bob pushed back his chair, stood up, and cleared his throat. "Thank you, thank you all. Lillian and I are very grateful for all the support you've given us. We're thrilled to be able to make our home here amongst you."

Lillian stood up, her arm through his. Her eyes glistened. "I am truly sorry for bringing my troubles here to you. Everyone has been so kind to us, so helpful. It's given us the strength to deal with it all." A tear ran down her face.

"Oh Lillian, its okay," said Susan, getting up and easing Lillian back into her chair.

Tom beamed and waved to the waitress. "Ronnie! We need a round here." He looked over at Bob and Lillian. "We'll set it up so it goes smooth with the capo guy. Lillian, go ahead and give the man a call, have him come out to Ken's Diner. Ralph and I will set it up with Ken and Allen. Don't let him come out before this Friday."

Bob and Lillian nodded. Lillian thanked him. The band had arrived and the place was filling up.

CHAPTER 16 VISITATION

Lillian looked at Bob, fearful of what she had to do. She picked up the telephone, and looking at the notepaper from Susan, dialed the Chicago number. She turned to Bob, smiled thinly.

"You'll be okay," encouraged Bob.

She heard the phone ring, and then again.

"Cappella Property Management, Mr. Cappella's office." It sounded like a young woman's voice.

"Hello. I…I'm Lillian Hoffner. I have a message. Mr. Cappella asked me to call him." She pressed her hand against her abdomen.

"Hello, Ms. Hoffner. We've been expecting your call."

She felt her stomach cramp up. Her hand trembled holding the phone. She put both hands on the handset.

Bob came up to her, put his arm around her shoulder, and eased her trembling.

After a pause, "This is Maria. I'm Mr. Cappella's secretary."

"Mr. Cappella is not in the office. However, he asked me to tell to you that he will be in Elk Creek to meet with you. He expects you to have the two items with you. He would like to meet at the airport, inside the terminal."

Lillian listened to every word, thinking of what he really meant.

"Ms. Hoffner?"

"I prefer to meet him in Elk Creek, at a place called Ken's Diner, at 7 o'clock Friday evening."

"He can try to manage that. I will call again if it is a problem."

"Okay."

"Mr. Cappella asked me to extend his apologies for the problems that you and your friends may have experienced from unauthorized actions by any of his people."

"Thank you."

"Mr. Cappella will be arriving in Camden Airport and will be at the meeting place at 7:00, unless I call you back."

"Yes…yes, Friday." She couldn't stop her hands from trembling.

"Thank you, Ms. Hoffner." The line went dead.

Bob took the phone from her trembling hands and placed it back on the table. He pulled her against him.

———

Vinny skidded to a stop behind the abandoned warehouse. Joey's call had frightened him; there had been panic in his voice. Joey had told him to bring the case with his piece and six extra clips. Then he had added to bring his toilet kit and a warm jacket. Where the hell were they going? They had been keeping out of sight. There was no way now that they could get the CD and book back, their best efforts had failed. Fear had replaced most of his anger and rage, neither one could see a way out.

Vinny climbed the steps to the loading dock, pulled the gun from his waist band, and pulled open the small access door. The loud screech of the rusty hinges announced his arrival.

"Put that goddamn thing away," growled Joey.

"Hey! Scared the shit outa me." Vinny pushed the gun back under his belt.

"Listen up. I heard from a guy that owes me, out at ExecuAir. He says that Cappella is flying out to Camden, Montana, at 4:30 *this* afternoon."

Vinny's eyes went wide. "Shit!"

"Yeah. Guy says Cappella ordered a car. He's gotta be going for the stuff. Why the hell else would *he* go out there? He coulda sent anyone."

"What're we gonna do? He gets that stuff, we're dead."

"That's why we're going out there *right now*. I got a guy'll fly us out there at 2 o'clock. I had to give him some big bucks. We go to Midway Airport; that's where he's at. So, get your stuff and toss it in my car. We're leaving now."

"Yeah, I got my case like you wanted. We got to take out the broad before he gets there."

"Yeah, no shit. If we don't," Joey hesitated for a moment, "then we take *him* out."

Vinny stared at Joey. A tremor went through him. This was their last chance.

———

Tom drove Ralph and Bob to Elk Creek and stopped in front of the fire station. A meeting with Allen had been set up for that morning. The three men entered the building and went back to Allen's office.

"It's a tight squeeze in here, but we shouldn't be long, just need to go over a few things," said Allen by means of introduction. He shook hands and indicated a chair for each.

"Okay, I'll check with all the flight services for Friday evening and see if there's an ExecuAir due in, and then see what car he drives. When they leave the airport I'll tail them at a respectable distance. That way he'll know we won't accept any funny business. When he gets into Elk Creek, I'll circle around and park a few doors behind them. That way I'll be ready to follow him back to the airport."

Tom raised his hand. "I've talked to Ken and he agrees to stay open until this is over. Not really open, but the lights will be on. Ralph and I will stay out of sight in the kitchen. Bob will bring Lillian to the diner at 7 o'clock and wait for her in the truck. When she leaves, they'll both go back to the ranch. When Cappella leaves, Ralph and I'll go home."

Allen looked at Bob, then at Tom. "You're both good with this?"

They nodded.

"Okay. That's the plan," said Allen. "There's really no reason for me to get in the act, since there are no wants or warrants on this guy. I'll just hang back, let them know I'm there. It sounds to me like this guy just wants this over with."

"That's what we're hoping," said Bob.

"I don't expect any trouble, but I'll be watching carefully from my car." Allen got up. "Okay? We got any questions?"

Everyone shook their head.

"No? Okay, I'm going down to Ken's Diner, get some lunch. Anyone want to join me?" asked Allen.

"Sure," said Tom rising from his chair. "How 'bout it guys?"

—

A white Lear jet stopped at the General Aviation terminal at Camden Airport a few minutes after five. Joey and Vinny moved quickly down the stairs, each gripping a black aluminum case. Inside the building they were met by a young woman at the Hertz counter. Joey signed for the SUV and was shown the way to the parking area. Joey spotted the gray Chevrolet SUV, the only one in the Hertz area. Joey started the motor while Vinny tucked their cases behind the seats.

Joey glanced in the mirror often as he headed south on County Road. "I've been thinking." He paused. "Like we talked on the plane, Cappella is going to meet the broad at some public place. But, he doesn't want to call unnecessary attention to himself, or be recognized by some guy that watches too much *Law and Order*."

"I know; we talked about it. We gotta get the broad first."

"Well, do we? Listen. We most likely got an hour and a half before he shows up. We can't run around here like a couple of idiots with our dicks cut off. That'd be a good way to catch someone's attention. No. What we can do is to wait for Cappella to show up, follow him to wherever the meeting place is, and after the exchange, we whack them."

"Kill Cappella? You gotta be shittin' me."

"What the hell else can we do? Huh? We won't know where the stuff is until they actually do the meeting. We nail 'em right there, get the stuff, and haul ass back to Camden. I can make a call, figure out how to get outa the country. If we run into trouble, we ditch the car and go to ground until I make arrangements."

"We kill Cappella, there'll be all hell to pay." Vinny sounded doubtful.

"Goddamnit! What the hell else we gonna do?" Joey glared at him, his face red. "This way at least, no one gets the stuff. Yeah, they'll figure it was us, but I don't plan on staying here. We'll go to Bolivia or Paraguay. We'll live alright."

Vinny was shaking his head slowly, looking down at his lap.

"What the hell else we gonna do?" shouted Joey. "Huh? Tell me!"

"Okay, I'm in. We *gotta* make this work," said Vinny.

—

Cappella looked at the mountains passing below. They'd be landing soon, and then he'd have one more hurdle before putting an end to his problem. There was no satisfactory way to explain the losses to the family, the mismanagement, the exposure in the press. Coming here was the only sure way to set this straight. He realized that Lillian had probably made a stupid error in judgment, and not a purposeful act of thievery or to humiliate the organization. He could forgive that, especially knowing Joey and Vinny for what they were. If he could just get the CD and book, then his life could go on without too much consequence. He hoped that Santos would be able to find the two assholes, and kill them by the time he got back.

The small ExecuAir jet landed at Camden a few minutes after 6:30 p.m. The pilot, co-pilot, and Frank Cappella, with his bodyguard, walked slowly down the retractable staircase. Cappella had a few words with the pilot, looked at his watch, and then indicated to his bodyguard to move into the terminal. At the Hertz counter, the woman looked puzzled.

"What?"

"Just rented an SUV to a couple other gentlemen from Chicago. It was maybe a couple hours ago."

"Family reunion." Frank didn't smile. A tremor went up his spine. He signed the forms and picked up the keys to a dark blue Mercury Grand Marquis.

She pointed. "It's parked in slot 23, out the far door."

He smiled. "Thank you."

Cappella looked around for his bodyguard. Billy was standing by the large windows overlooking the tarmac, a shiny aluminum case and a computer bag at his feet. His eyes swept the corridor slowly.

"Let's go. We might have a problem."

"What's up, boss?" asked Billy.

They walked to the end of the corridor, through the doors, and into the Hertz parking lot.

"Number 23. Here's the keys."

Billy took them and hurried ahead to open the rear door for Cappella. When he was seated, Billy put his case on the floor and closed the door. He looked at his boss; saw the frown on his brow. He got in behind the wheel and backed out of the parking spot, then turned toward the exit gate. A minute later, they were on County Road heading toward Elk Creek.

"Something wrong, boss?"

"I think we're going to have company when we get there. We're likely to have some trouble. Seems Joey and this Vinny guy are here," said Cappella.

"I know 'em, boss."

"They'll try to whack us. You can deal with that?"

"I can deal with it." Billy glanced at the mirror and frowned. "We've got company."

"It's probably the cop that was parked back there following us. Just stay within the speed limit."

"Okay. There's a place called Randolph coming up."

"Yeah, drive right through it. Elk Creek is three miles past it."

—

Allen watched the dark blue Mercury Grand Marquis as it left through the airport exit gate and then started to follow it. An hour earlier, the Hertz salesperson had confirmed that Cappella had reserved a vehicle. Now, as the big car passed by slowly, he started his engine. He kept a couple hundred feet separation to the blue car until they were on County Road, then increased the separation to 500 feet. They would know that he was back there.

"Dispatch. Allen."

"Allen, what's your 20?"

"County Road, southbound at the airport."

"Do you have your party?"

"Party in sight and rolling."

"10-4."

—

Cappella didn't turn around to look; he would have been more surprised if the cop hadn't been there. He could have sent Lorenz on this trip. He would have done well. But, it was important to be out of town this particular evening while Santos took care of the renegades and put an end to this crisis. But now, he realized, it was going to turn out differently.

He wondered whether he should have put Santos back on the street. He had been very good at it, smart and deadly, but he wasn't a youngster anymore. He had wanted to reward Santos by bringing him inside, a nice office, an easier life, but now he had to rethink it. Hadn't the trouble with those two renegades started about the time that he took Santos off the street? No one had dared to cross Santos, not then.

Cappella hadn't taken lightly the warning from his boss. His old mentor, now living in a nursing home, had called, saying that Cappella would only be given a short time to fix things, and that he could do nothing at this point to help him with the family. He would have to retrieve the stolen records; the information they contained would be essential to his being able to set things right.

"Boss, the cop is still behind us."

"Its okay, Billy. That's Randolph ahead. Watch your speed."

He wondered where the two assholes were. Had they beat him to Lillian? Had they recovered the stuff? No, he had to think positive, had to stay alert. If those two were here, it was because they had found out he was coming to get the CD and book. Was he walking into an already bad scene, the stuff gone and maybe someone shot, and police to greet him? What if they waited for him to arrive, to be sure of the place for the pick up? That made sense. Hiding somewhere along this road. Watching. The cop behind him would give him time. The sun had set but there was still some daylight left. He would make it there alright. But then what? He wouldn't alarm Billy yet.

"Is that Elk Creek coming up?"

"Yeah boss. It sure don't look like much."

"Okay. Now pay attention. We're looking for Ken's Diner."

"I see it. On the left, just ahead."

"Keep going. Drive all the way through town, then make a U-turn and come back to park in front.

"Got it."

Cappella wondered how things had gotten so out of whack? Where had those two bastards stashed all the money they had skimmed? The family would want to know. They might suspect *him*. The CD and record book would be important, would probably have account numbers and passwords. His raging anger had abated some over the last week. His mentor had advised him that he would have to put it aside, keep a clear head, do what he had to do, and do it quickly.

"Cop's still behind us, boss."

"Take it easy, Billy. Just turn here, nice and slow. Make the U-turn and head back."

"Jeez, people live in this place?" Billy shook his head.

"They're just different kind of folks."

"That cop, he made a U-turn. He's behind us," said Billy.

"I expected that. Don't worry about it."

—

Joey had seen Cappella drive by from where he was parked, just south of the airport. The big car, a driver, he was sure it was him. Just in time, he saw the sheriff's car come along, some distance behind Cappella. He put some space between himself and the sheriff, and held well back as they proceeded toward Randolph and Elk Creek.

"Why's the sheriff following him?"

"Joey shrugged. "Don't know. Maybe the broad asked him to."

"Could get complicated."

"We'll see where they go when they get to Elk Creek. Then we'll park on a back street and move in on foot. We'll size up the situation."

"Yeah, okay. Maybe we'll survive this." Vinny didn't sound hopeful.

"Goddamn it! You want to live, get focused. Whatever happens will happen real fast."

—

They were almost there. *Where the hell are these guys?* Cappella wondered. An ambush? A gunfight would produce all kinds of cops and witnesses. He felt a tinge of fear gnawing at him. He knew that Billy would be up to the task. The two of them had grown up together. They had always watched each other's back; at school and later, in the business, Billy had been at his side. Not a genius, but loyal to the marrow of his bones. But things could go wrong. The two renegades were running on empty, they had nothing to lose. Where the hell were they?

He had been hopeful of being back in the airplane in an hour. Now he had his doubts. Lillian would be cooperative. Why wouldn't she be? He had brought a ten grand bundle, but he didn't think he would need it. Lillian had impressed him as a sensible and supportive wife when he had met her, a classy lady, someone much too good for Joey. He had been tempted, but realized the danger and dismissed his urges. Lorenz and Santos told him that she had never talked to the FBI or the DA. That had been Joey's paranoia. He had no doubt she was scared. *I'll try to make this easy for her*, he mused.

"Here's the diner, boss. A real greasy spoon. No one in it."

"There's sure to be someone in there. The woman will be along any minute."

"That cop is parked a little ways behind us."

"Uh-huh. Here she comes now. That truck just went by is stopping."

"Boss, I don't like this, don't like you goin' in there by yourself."

"I'll be alright, Billy. Do not get out of the car. Keep your piece hidden away. Do as I tell you and we'll be okay."

"You sure about this boss?"

"I'll be back shortly."

——

Joey walked rapidly down a narrow service alley to peer out onto the main street. Vinny came up behind him and tried to look past Joey's shoulder.

"That him?" whispered Vinny.

"Yeah. Cop's parked a few doors to the right."

"How we do this?"

"When they come outa the diner we go over there and finish this."

"Gotta get them both," mumbled Vinny.

"Get back, truck coming." He pushed Vinny back into the shadows as the old red hay truck slowed and pulled to a stop just past Ken's Diner.

—

Cappella opened the back door of the car and got out, taking his laptop computer. He pushed the door closed, and walked to the diner entrance. The door opened easily when he nudged it with his shoulder. The diner was quiet, expect for some electrical humming noises from the kitchen. He was sure someone would be watching. He took a seat in a booth against the wall, away from the window.

—

Lillian kissed Bob and got out of the truck with the bag holding the CD and record book. It was the same bag she had taken from Vinny's safe. She walked quickly to the diner, pushed the door open, and stepped inside, her heart pounding. She saw him sitting in the booth, a laptop open on the table. He got out of his seat, and motioned for her to sit.

"Good evening, Lillian." A small smile appeared at the corners of his mouth. "I think we should have had this meeting some time ago."

She recognized Cappella immediately. He hadn't changed noticeably. She smiled thinly, nodding.

"Thank you for agreeing to meet me. This unfortunate event has been troubling for both of us. I do apologize for what happened to you and your friend. It was not my intention."

She nodded. "I got angry and frightened and acted foolishly."

He looked calmly at her for a moment. "If you brought what I need, I can put an end to this business with the family, and I can guarantee no harm will come to you."

Lillian nodded, her lips trembled slightly. "I…I never betrayed anyone. I was very angry the way that Vinny was treating me." She looked at his face. It didn't reveal anything.

"Vinny is a pig. Joey, I trusted - a made man. This thing is on me. It should not have happened." Cappella looked calmly into her face.

"I couldn't stay with Joey - paranoid about everything, thinking I was talking to the FBI. I never betrayed him or anyone." She suddenly felt tired.

"I never believed that you talked to anyone. I think those two had been stuffing the powder up their noses for so long that their brains didn't work right."

She nodded, looked at her lap. "I have the CD and book here. There are no copies."

"There is a policeman out there. Are you wearing a wire?"

Her eyes widened. "No." Her lip trembled. "Do you want to…"

He shook his head. "No. If there are any copies – I'll be under a lot of pressure to clean this up. You understand me?"

"Yes. There are no copies."

"That cop out there, is he going to be a problem for me?"

"No. My friends are nervous, is all."

He looked at her for a few seconds, and then asked calmly, "May I take a look at it?"

She handed him the bag. He flipped through the record book, then set it aside to pick up the CD, and inserted it into his computer. He opened the file listing, and scanned it from top to bottom without saying a word. He opened several files and closed them again. He made an encrypted copy of the CD to his hard drive.

Cappella looked up and met Lillian's gaze. "There is a lot on this CD. It will go a long way to explaining things."

"Take it," she said softly.

"I could maybe help you out, give you a few grand?"

She shook her head.

He put the CD and the record book in the bag. He looked at her. "Lillian, if there are no copies of this stuff, this'll be the end if it."

"I'm glad for that."

"We'll leave now. I imagine your friends are getting nervous."

She nodded and got up from her seat. "Good night."

He nodded and followed her to the door.

Lilian pushed open the door and welcomed the cool air of dusk on her face. She turned right toward Bob and the truck. When she saw movement across the street, she stopped and stared.

"Vinny," she gasped. The shock to her shoulder came as she heard the shot. She fell back against Cappella. He staggered and the second shot grazed his head. They both fell to the sidewalk. She tried to scream, but there was no sound. Then she felt Cappella's powerful grip around her waist as he dragged her back into the doorway of the adjacent business, a dress shop. A cry escaped her as she felt the sharp pain in her shoulder. Cappella propped her against the display window of the entry way and rose to a crouch.

Billy was part way out of the car, his gun resting on the window edge as he fired. Two quick shots and Cappella saw Vinny drop to the ground. He glanced to his left; the deputy sheriff was out of his car. A movement to the right caught Cappella's eye. Bob dove out of the passenger side of the truck and ran at a crouch toward Cappella.

"Where is she? Where's Lillian?" he shouted.

"Get down! She's here in the doorway." Frank pointed to where she lay propped against the glass, her left shoulder now red with blood.

"Lillian!" Bob dropped to his knees in the doorway.

Billy fired again. Cappella grabbed his computer case and lunged to the car, scrambling into the back seat. Billy, back in the car, slammed the accelerator to the floor and pulled away leaving a long squeal of rubber.

—

When they heard the first shot Tom and Ralph burst out of the kitchen and ran toward the door. Tom saw a man on the far side of the street angling to the left. He grabbed Ralph and pulled him down to the floor, below the level of the window sills.

"We got to get to Bob and Lillian!" yelled Ralph.

Ralph struggled to get up. Tom gripped him hard.

"No! There's a shooter coming across the street. Allen is out there somewhere. Go to the phone out back. Call the sheriff's office. Hurry.".

Other shots rang out. Tom crouched down while Ralph was on the phone with the dispatcher. He returned soon to squat next to Tom.

"They heard from Allen. They're sending help." Then his eyes glistened, "Oh God, Bob and Lillian." His voiced trailed off. "What can we do?"

—

Allen crouched on the curb side of his SUV. He had radioed that there were shots fired, people injured and an officer under attack. How many were there? He saw someone lying in the road beyond where Cappella had been parked. Had he heard something, a sixth sense? He turned to catch a glimpse of a man darting from a building across the street trying to come up from behind.

"Oh, shit."

He crouched and ran toward the doorway where he saw Lillian being dragged and Bob disappeared. He knew that Lillian had been shot. As he got to the doorway where Lillian and Bob were crouched, he staggered. The shot felled him on his right side, gun dropped from his hand, and he slid down against the window, toppling to his side. Shock and pain swept over him, and he lost consciousness.

Panic gripped Bob as he saw Allen take a hit and drop. Bob reached for Allen, dragging him by his arm pits, getting his exposed legs into the meager shelter of the doorway. Another shot rang out. Pain seared through his side. He tried to focus. Where was the shooter? They were sitting ducks.

Bob reached over Allen and picked up the pistol and then fell back, sitting against the wall. The pain in his side was now excruciating. He pulled up his knees, resting the gun between them, squinting into the darkness. He saw him then, coming along the street side of the vehicles in a crouch. Bob gripped the pistol tightly, aiming it at the crouched figure. Bob fired. The shot thundered in the small alcove. The man stopped, leaned against a car. He turned toward Bob, trying to raise the gun. Bob pulled the trigger again. The gun fell out of the man's hand. He slipped along the hood and fell. He did not move.

Bob's eyes were not seeing much. He felt himself letting go as the sound of sirens filtered into his hearing. He fell across Lillian's legs.

"Bob! Bob!" screamed Lillian. She tried to reach him but couldn't move her arm. She lay her head back against the window, sobbing.

—

"You're hurt." Billy cast a quick look over his shoulder. "You're bleeding."

Cappella put his handkerchief against the wound on his temple. "Keep going Billy. I don't want to be stopped."

"Okay." He cast another glance back to Cappella. "You're hurt boss. Should I find a doctor?"

"No. To the airport. Get me on that plane."

"I'll get you there."

"Billy, when we get there, make sure and bring the case with you. Don't leave any shells in the car. Look under your seat. Okay?"

"Okay. I gotta get you to that plane first."

"Don't get stopped, Billy."

"Oh, shit, cops coming this way."

"Don't even look at them – just keep going. We'll be okay."

—

The street was jammed with sheriff's cars and two ambulances from Camden as well as the unit from Elk Creek's volunteer EMTs. Sheriff Crawford and two of his deputies had secured the street, verifying that the two gunmen were no longer a threat. He rushed to the front of the diner where he saw people down and blood running from the entry.

Lillian was conscious. He checked her wound, a through and through. He gave her a clean handkerchief to press against it. All three ambulances backed up to the store front. The EMTs urgently performed triage. Crawford saw that Allen and Bob, both unconscious, were bleeding profusely. He was told that Bob's wound didn't look good, as the bullet was still in him.

Crawford felt sick. What the hell had happened? He watched as the deputies documented the scene of the gun battle. He told one of the deputies to take photos of the victims. People were coming out of Larry's Bar and Grill and crowding ever closer to the crime scene. He ordered a deputy to tape off the whole area, curb to curb. On the radio, he asked dispatch to send out the CSU team immediately. Another deputy arrived. The ambulance crew started triage.

The EMT team from Camden worked feverishly on Bob and Allen. Radio and instrumentation contact with ER at the hospital was maintained as

EMTs stabilized them and worked to bring them out of shock. It was another fifteen minutes before they were ready to transport them to Camden. As the two ambulances departed, the sheriff looked at the scene. How close to losing all three had they come? He had found Allen's gun at Bob's side. Had he held them off? A deputy walked up to him, flipping through a notebook.

"Sheriff, the two in the street have Chicago addresses on their licenses. We also found a car a block away they had rented and there was a gun case in it. Their pockets had several extra clips."

"You got names on these two?"

"Yeah. The one up here in the street is Vincent DiCosta. The guy by the curb is Joseph DiCosta. You know 'em?"

He shook his head. "Never heard of 'em."

"Detectives coming?"

The sheriff nodded. "You wait here for them. I'm going to talk to some of these folks, see if we have any witnesses.

—

Tom and Ralph stepped out of the diner cautiously. The shooting had stopped. Tom restrained Ralph from impetuously running toward where he thought Bob and Lillian were.

"I gotta see them! Where are they?"

Tom held onto Ralph's arm. "No! Wait. Make sure the shooters are gone."

Ralph broke free and started toward where he thought Bob and Lillian had gone. Tom followed on his heals. Suddenly a deputy stepped in front of them, gun drawn.

"Stop! Who the hell are you two?" The surprise and embarrassed shock showed on his young face.

"Hey, we were in the back of the diner. I'm Tom Bauer, he's Ralph Stehling."

The deputy saw the sheriff approaching as he was about to call him on the radio. "Sheriff, these two guys just came outa the diner."

"It's okay, deputy. I know 'em." Crawford shook his head. "Just what the hell you two doing in there?"

Tom answered. "We were in the back, in the kitchen. Lillian was meeting with this Cappella guy and we were just back there watching, in case something went wrong. When they left, we were going to leave, too. Then all hell broke loose. We didn't know if the shooters were right outside or where."

Ralph asked, "Where are Lillian and Bob? What happened to them?"

"EMTs are working on them right now."

Ralph looked at Tom. "I gotta see them."

Crawford shook his head. "No. They're going to the hospital. You can go there in a while. In the meantime, I want your statement."

Crawford took out his notebook.

—

Cappella opened his eyes. His head throbbed. He touched where Billy had bandaged him.

"The crew okay with this?

"Yeah, boss. I gave them a little extra like you said. They'll taxi to the front of Dexter Aviation and let us off. Maybe we can avoid interference."

Billy handed him the secure phone. "Santos is holding for you."

"Mike?"

"Where are you Frank?"

"In the air. Call me back, code-06. I'm switching now."

Cappella's phone rang about forty seconds later with the scrambler engaged.

"Mike, you hear me okay?"

"Yeah, Frank. I'm good here," replied Santos. "Did your trip go okay?"

"No, not okay. But I've got what I came for. You didn't get a hold of those two, did you?"

"No. I looked everywhere and called up every favor I had coming. Nobody would give them up."

"They weren't there, Mike. They were here."

"Holy shit. What happened?"

"First off, we got a leak somewhere. You might check at ExecuAir. Somebody tipped them off, and they got here a couple hours ahead of me."

"I'll find the leak. What happened out there?"

"I met the woman and she gave me the stuff. But when we left the place, those two pieces of shit ambushed us."

"You get hurt?"

"Yeah. I'll be okay." He didn't say what he was thinking, that Lillian falling against him had most likely saved his life.

"I'll get old Doc Springer to look at it."

"Yeah, fine. Our two dirt bags are no more. We got one of 'em, and I heard on the car radio the other's also on the slab."

"Good goddamn riddance. You get everything you needed?"

"Yeah. They kept the skim at Seaman's Mercantile Bank in Aruba. Anyway, I got all the account numbers. I'll let Lorenz figure it all out."

"Frank, we gonna have trouble…the law, I mean?"

"I don't know, but listen. Be in a car by yourself at the Dexter Aviation gate, that's where we'll de-plane; *not* at ExecuAir. I want you to get the hell out of there immediately and take me to one of the safe houses. Make sure it's empty, I don't want company. I need to hide this stuff until my meeting."

"Sure. Okay. I'll set it up right now. Are the feds going to be looking for you?"

"I don't know, but if they nab me when I land, get hold of my attorney. He'll know what to do."

"I'll be there."

"I gotta be in front of the family next week. Maybe we can survive this without too much of a shitstorm."

"I've been thinking, Frank." There was a slight pause. "I should go out in the field again, tighten up the ship, as it were. This shouldn't have happened."

"We'll talk tomorrow. Come by the office in the afternoon."

"Okay."

CHAPTER 17 NEW BEGINNING

Tom and Ralph spent three days at the hospital and another at the DA's office. There were interviews with the sheriff, the detectives, and the DA, while the DA tried to get to the bottom of things. Lillian's condition improved rapidly and she was sent home the following afternoon. Allen, too, had a brief stay, before an extended medical leave while he went through the prescribed rehab process.

Bob's wound had become infected and he was hospitalized for five days. Afterward, Lillian kept him in bed and watched over him constantly. He started to walk again after ten days, slowly regaining his strength. Lillian continued to experience pain in her shoulder, but didn't complain. They held each other often, grateful for a new lease on life.

Tim McGuire managed to annoy everyone with his penchant for getting a story, the biggest one of his young career. Meanwhile, the DA announced that no charges were being filed against anyone; the perpetrators had paid for their crimes with their lives, and everyone else was acting in self-defense. Lillian refused to name Cappella at all, even as a co-conspirator.

—

Ralph and Susan drove back from Camden with the newly-married couple in the back seat. Susan turned to Lillian and Bob. "That was a nice ceremony. The judge is a good man."

"Thanks for standing with us," said Lillian.

"I couldn't let you two go alone. No telling what kind of trouble you would have gotten into." Ralph grinned. "Besides, gave me a good reason to wash my truck. Of course, I almost couldn't get into my suit, bought it for Liz's graduation."

"Oh, Ralph!" Susan punched his arm.

She turned to Lillian. "It was nice to stop at St. Anne's. Father Macmillan seemed real happy to bless you in your marriage."

"Bob is not Catholic, but I just wanted to have the blessing. I'm glad he did that for us," said Lillian. "He didn't have to, being divorced and all."

Ralph turned partly around to look at them. "Hey folks, we're stopping at Larry's." He had a grin on his face.

It was only 2 o'clock in the afternoon and yet most of the nearby parking places were occupied. Ralph made a U-turn and parked near Ken's Diner.

"Looks like a few folks showed up, doesn't it?" Ralph winked at Susan.

"Sure seems like it," she said.

"What have you guys done?" asked Bob.

"Us? Nothing. Well, here we are." Ralph stepped ahead and opened the door. A sign taped to the door read: *Private Party, closed until 6 p.m.*

Larry looked around. All was ready. He and the staff with the help of Tom and Karen had decorated the lounge for the reception. Friends of Lillian and Bob from the ranch and in town were seated at the tables covered with white linen and silver service. A large wedding cake stood prominently at the head table. Gifts were stacked on the table behind it against the wall.

Larry turned from the small window in the front door. "Hey! Here they come!"

A hush fell over the crowd. Then the front door swung open. A chorus of cheers erupted as Lillian and Bob stepped into the lounge. Good wishes and congratulations were offered. Larry and the wait staff brought out trays of food. All drinks were on the house. Lillian and Bob beamed.

Tom looked up. "Lillian, I received this at the ranch this morning. I brought it along." He handed Lillian an envelope. "No return address, but it's got a Chicago postmark." He raised his eyebrows.

Lillian frowned and reached across the table for the envelope. She looked at Bob, he shrugged. She put a finger nail under the flap and pried it open. Ten 100 bills fell onto the table when she withdrew the card. The card was embossed with a gold motif. Inside was a hand written message. Lillian stared at the card. No one spoke. Ralph looked at Bob, then at Tom.

Finally, Tom asked, "What's it say?"

She handed the card to Tom. He read it, looked up, and then read it aloud.

I was saddened to hear of the injuries you and your fiancé sustained during my visit. I offer my sincere apologies. I offer, too, my best wishes for your marriage to a real stand-up guy.

F.

There was a moment of silence, and then smiles broke out all around. The card made its way around the table, finally ending with Bob.

Tom raised his glass. "To a real stand-up guy!"

THE END

www.ingramcontent.com/pod-product-compliance
Lightning Source LLC
Chambersburg PA
CBHW070755160726
48004CB00001B/201